BONES AND THE BEREAVED

COPYRIGHT © 2026 RACHAEL RANTZ

ALL RIGHTS RESERVED. NO PART OF THIS BOOK MAY BE REPRODUCED, SCANNED, OR TRANSMITTED IN ANY PRINTED, ELECTRONIC, OR MECHANICAL, INCLUDING PHOTOCOPYING, RECORDING, OR ANY INFORMATION STORAGE AND RETRIEVAL SYSTEM, WITHOUT PERMISSION IN WRITING FROM THE PUBLISHER. PLEASE DO NOT PARTICIPATE OR ENCOURAGE PIRACY OF COPYRIGHTED MATERIALS IN VIOLATION OF THE AUTHOR'S RIGHTS. FOR PERMISSION REQUESTS, PLEASE ADDRESS 5 TWO PRESS, LLC.

FOR INFORMATION, ADDRESS
5 TWO PRESS, LLC
PO BOX 535
CARSON CITY, NV 89701

HELLO@5TWOPRESS.COM

5 TWO PRESS, LLC
A NEVADA COMPANY

THE INFORMATION GIVEN IN THIS BOOK SHOULD NOT BE TREATED AS A SUBSTITUTE FOR PROFESSIONAL MEDICAL ADVICE; ALWAYS CONSULT A MEDICAL PRACTITIONER. ANY USE OF INFORMATION IN THIS BOOK IS AT THE READER'S DISCRETION AND RISK. NEITHER THE AUTHOR NOR THE PUBLISHER CAN BE HELD RESPONSIBLE FOR ANY LOSS, CLAIM, OR DAMAGE ARISING OUT OF THE USE, OR MISUSE, OF THE SUGGESTIONS MADE, THE FAILURE TO TAKE MEDICAL ADVICE OR FOR ANY MATERIAL ON THIRD-PARTY WEBSITES.

ISBN: 979-8-9998932-0-8

COVER DESIGNED BY: RACHAEL RANTZ
NAMES: RANTZ, RACHAEL, AUTHOR + CREATOR
TITLE: BONES AND THE BEREAVED

BONES AND THE BEREAVED

A creative portal for leaning into the heaviness of grief deep inside our bones.

BY RACHAEL RANTZ

A NEVADA COMPANY

This book is dedicated to my husband, soul mate, and best friend, Brian. Thank you for choosing me to walk you home. You have carried me as much as I have carried you. You will now and forever be the love of my life and my greatest teacher.

CONTENTS

FORWARD + INTRODUCTION - VII

FLOWER MEDICINE - 1

Flower Drying / Whispers Though the Flowers
Flower Frog / Contemplation with a Flower
Medicine Bottles / Medicine Mantras
Crown of Love / Being with the Body
Marigold Garland / Sun + Shadow
Memorial Petals / Elemental Casting Invocations
Remembrance Altar / Impermanence Practice
Momento Mori / Flickers of Finite

GRIEF - 33

Mourning Handkerchief / Sitting with Your Tears
Grief Tree / Seasons of Grief
Shatter and Release / Grief Support
Sunsetting Strands / Unfeigned Feelings
Mourning Band / Band of Anchors
Grief Stones / Sounding Breathwork for Primal Grief
Words of Woe / Tending Through Naming
Grief Garden / Soil + Soul

PRAYERS - 62

Prayer Beads / Holding Prayer
Protection Bracelet / Mourning Movement
Sigil / Charging Your Sigil
Prayer Flags / Breathless Blessings
Bubble Wand / Communicating with the Other Side
Travel Altar / Grief-cation
Vigil Votive / Keeping Vigil
Lovey / Comfort Care for the End of Life

LEGACY - 95

Impression Medallion / Hand Remembrance Meditation
Love Letter / An Unsent Letter
Blanket Coat / Mourning Wear Meditation
Family Tree / Reflections From Family Roots
Photo Album / Embodied Memory Practice
Journal / Daily Reflections and Reminiscing Writing Prompts
End of Life Photography / Acts of Observations + Reflections
Keepsake Case / Reminiscence Visualization

DEATH CONTEMPLATION - 128

Send-Off Shrine / Holding Sacred Silence
Crossing the Veil / Into the Ether
Death Cleaning / Words of Release
Death Nest / Calling in Comforts
Liminal Soundscape / Humming
Final Rest Eye Pillow / Corpse Pose Meditation
Eulogy / My Husband's Eulogy

FINAL FEELINGS - 158

IN GRATITUDE - 162

BOOK RECOMMENDATIONS - 163

FORWARD

> Learning to befriend the darkness of us is holding space where we are able to do the necessary work of metabolizing sorrow.
>
> Francis Weller
> The Wild Edge of Sorrow

My husband and I navigated the waves of the death portal for over four years. We were told it would be weeks to months of his diseases progression to end of life. He was slowly dying and part of myself was passing away alongside him.

Brian and I met when we were fourteen, just starting high school. We quickly became best friends, bonded even more deeply when we discovered our birthdays were only a day apart. Even as friends, our love ran deeper. Finally, senior year he asked me to be his girlfriend while we sat in my parked car up at Windy Hill. We were committed for a while but our paths eventually merged into different routes as we needed to separate to experience our own growth in different ways, in different cities. We kept in touch over the years and when our paths crossed again a decade later we knew it was our time. We rekindled our relationship in 2019, and everything that followed felt written in the stars.

Brian was a bicycle messenger in San Francisco. It was a dream he had always wanted and finally achieved in the big city. On a Thursday afternoon in 2020 he was riding home after a delivery and he was hit by a car. He suffered major broken facial bones, a stroke, and a traumatic brain injury that triggered the progression of a rare genetic disease he was diagnosed with at a young age, Adrenoleukodystrophy (ALD) and Addisons Disease. It is the same disease his younger brother died from when they were young boys. In Spring 2021 his neurologist said his progression to a vegetative state and end of life would take weeks to months. When we got him home I told him I wanted to get married and he replied, "I thought that since we were fourteen."

We went from palliative care, to an intimate wedding, a treehouse honeymoon, and then onto hospice. I entered into a caregiver and death doula role as reality of approaching death set in. Little losses arose as his disease progressed at a slow pace. His speech was the first thing the disease began to affect. Loss of words, the inability to express himself, answer questions, and ultimately his voice faded completely. I carry the date of his final "I love you" permanently marked over my heart.

His physical body began to weaken as he went from walking with a cane to receiving the aid of a wheelchair. The wheelchair went from a low back to a high reclining back as the strength in his core declined and he couldn't hold himself seated upright any longer. He needed support bathing, feeding, toileting, and simply moving from position to position. It fell to me to be his strength. I became the one who listened for what he couldn't express and give voice to what he could no longer say. I dedicated myself to keeping him safe, clean, and comfortable.

In the midst of the declines we found solace in the craft. Prior to his terminal diagnosis we were both immensely artistic. Brian was a writer, poet, glassblower, and musician. I used to teach art meditation workshops and host crafting gatherings in our communities. We would crochet, sew, and create beautiful gifts for one another. Even after his accident, he still gave his best effort to help contribute and support the pieces I was creating. As his physical and mental strength diminished I crafted alongside him as he rested.

Four days after our four year wedding anniversary Brian took his final breaths. Hand in hand, this was our last act of love for each other - walking life out. He labored through transition with grace and the strength of a warrior. He held on to every ounce of life force that remained in his body to gift us time.

Our intention was to seal in the sacred. Our death nest became a love bubble. It brings me comfort knowing he experienced a good death. He knew he was loved, held, safe, and not alone. It was a blessing and a privilege to witness him ascend slowly.

I am and forever will be so proud of him

This book was birthed alongside our death journey. As much as I dreamed of having a child with him, this book became our shared creation together. A part of him, a part of me, woven together. Both of us drew breath into each piece, infusing it with our combined energies.

Dying can be sacred and beautiful. I'm humbled to share a little piece of our journey with you.

BONES

Bones are the representation of life, death, and the coexistence in-between. After death, our skeleton is the body's final form, sometimes returned to ash. Some believe it is our bones that house the soul and carry stories from our past, present, and future.

Sorrow settles deep beneath the surface, woven into our being. It is a deep all-embracing experience we bear throughout our body. It can feel bone crushing and marrow deep. If the grief is not allowed to move through the body the energy may settle leaving a sense of profound heaviness.

As the reality set in that my husband was dying anticipatory grief planted a seed rooting deeply into my body, reaching the bone. As my grief grew my body began to feel weighed down. The physical heaviness of the weight anchored me deep in muddy waters. Despite my efforts to rise above, I was only trudging through.

Creating pulled me out of the muck. It became a tool that guided me out of the darkness allowing my grief to finally flow away from stagnation into a place of being present and sitting with my sorrow. Carrying my grief softened into wearing it with peace and gratitude.

BEREAVED

The bereaved are those in deep sorrow from being deprived of a loved one through a deeply felt loss, especially attributed to a loved one's death. The bereaved exude raw feelings of becoming desolate, lonesome, and bare.

Bereavement describes the period after a death in which people who cared about them are in mourning. In society, it has become an expectation that mourning has a timeframe. We await an end to our despair. In reality, once grief enters, it becomes a lifelong companion.

In my own experience, not everyone will be in a place emotionally to sit in sacred space with the mourning. If a profound loss has not been experienced it may feel unfathomable to walk alongside the grieving. At first, I struggled with the absence of friends and family during the time in our death nest, but I've come to see they were holding us from afar, present in an unseen way. That knowing comforts me now.

When voicing my sadness to my therapist she told me about the 5% theory. She said if you were drowning in the ocean 5% of your village would run out there braving the deep waters and save you. 15% of your village would be waiting at low tide to carry you back to shore. 80% of your village will be on the beach ready to help pick you back up. Even if those you expect to be there aren't, that doesn't mean they won't be there in time to come.

THE CREATOR

The creator archetype dwells within us all. It is the part of you that aspires to make something come alive with deep intention. We all posses creative instincts. Makers transform vision into reality. Whether through the meals that nourish loved ones or the spaces that shelter and hold them. There is quiet artistry even in the simplest act of being.

It is my hope that pieces of these pages inspire you and call on you to recreate it with your own vision. May the offerings in this book encourage and awaken your own creative flow. They are not meant to be fabricated the same as I have done. Let these works be a source to lean on, adapt, and make your own. When complete, your creations will carry the essence of you.

SIMPLE INSTRUCTIONS

Each piece contains simple instructions which I invite you to draw inspiration from. Imagine a collection of projects, each waiting to spark your creativity. A craft catches your eye and you try to recreate it in your own way. Sometimes there are very elaborate step by step instructions. Other times there are no instructions at all and you need to improvise. This book is the in-between.

These loose instructions are to be taken lightly. They are merely suggestions. If you feel called to do something a different way, do it. Be intuitive. Go with your own creative flow. Find your own way and move freely. This is your journey of self expression. These pages are only a gentle guide that hopes a project brings you a sense of peace along your journey here.

CRAFT COMPLETION EXERCISES

At the end of each craft you'll find pages veiled in darkness. These black pages hold craft completion exercises offering a deeper connection to your creation or journey. These simple, intentional practices done after a crafting session can offer closure, reflection, and deeper meaning to the creative process. These practices weave together breathwork, meditation, guided writings, and end of life guidance. Each offering was designed specifically for and bears a relationship to the craft it follows. They are intended to be read with slowness and space to pause and reflect.

Integrating these exercises afterwards adds an additional layer of reflection and inner stillness that brings more depth to the experience. It helps connect the physical act of making with deeper intentions behind the project.

MEDITATIVE ART

To meditate is to bring your awareness to your mind and body while creating a sense of calmness. As you begin to focus on your breath you awaken to the here and now. Mindfulness occurs when we sit with presence, setting aside discernment. As your thoughts begin to arise you learn to control the mind, concentrate, and redirect attention while encouraging relaxation and self expression.

Meditative art is a mindful flow that uses art as a guide into a healing creative journey. The focus is the process of creating rather than the end result. It doesn't need to look perfect, it needs to be authentic. I mourn the creations never made, held back by the need to be flawless. When we let go of perfection it leads to therapeutic and calming benefits. The art is not meant to be without fault. The practice is intended to find moments of peace, flow, and freedom.

How to incorporate meditation with art

- Mindfully prepare a space that invites comfort and creative expression.
- Arrive in presence.
- Set an intention or dedication for your practice.
- Allow your breath to anchor you in the moment.
- Tune into the sensations in your body.
- Tune into the quiet stream of your inner dialogue.
- Observe your thoughts without judgement.
- Honor the pauses as much as the progress.
- Reflect on the intention behind the time you spent here.

After a crafting session, you may choose to sit quietly, holding your finished piece, and take a few deep breaths. Reflect silently on any feelings that surfaced while making it.

What did this process teach me?
What am I releasing?
What am I honoring?
How does this piece reflect a part of me right now?

DEATH ARTISTRY

Death artistry delves into themes of mortality. Creating art with the theme of death and dying can be profoundly healing and meditative as it allows us to face, process, and express emotions tied to loss and impermanence. As we explore the realities of mortality with openness we begin to demystify and destigmatize the experience. Art provides a safe space to confront the reality of death without judgement or fear. Instead of avoiding death, we can begin to engage with it intentionally, which can lead to greater acceptance and peace.

Final thought, creating death-related art does not glorify death, it gives space to witness it and affirms its presence. It honors the complexity of being alive. It allows us to befriend the inevitable, to find beauty in endings, and transform pain into something expressive, sacred, and even healing.

CONNECTION WITH OTHERS

Death-themed art can foster communal healing. You are not alone in this journey. Your experience is shared, even if it feels isolating. Crafting in community can help people realize we are not alone in our feelings. It becomes a shared language for grief and remembrance, offering collective release and empathy. Community crafting is a living practice, molded by those who show up. A circle of makers may take many shapes. Your craft circle might begin intimately with just a few people and naturally extend into a wider community.

In addition to experiencing four years of anticipatory grief with my husband I also had to cope with several additional profound family deaths'. My mother had two brothers die within a months time of each other and my 15 year old cat, Eleanor, died just a year before Brian. In collective grief my mother and I would share Sundays crafting, moving through the sadness, and sharing space. It became a Sacred Sunday, in a way. So, you'll notice some projects will showcase not just my husband, but of other ancestors as well.

SUPPLIES

Think of the supplies as gentle guidance. I leaned into what I felt connected to, drawing mostly from what I had available. Use your creative instincts and choose what materials call to you.

For instance, the Medicine Bottle craft suggests using pressed flowers, but you might feel drawn to cutting out affirming words and images from old magazines to decorate it instead. Each project is an invitation for you to find your own inspiration. Think of these projects as seeds, you get to decide how they grow.

Suggestions for sourcing supplies

- Source supplies you can use more than once.

- Shop second hand.

- Passed down items are great ways to give new life to something that had once belonged to a loved one.

- Improvise. If you don't have something specific take a moment and think if you have something similar you could use or do it a different way.

- Plan a crafting gathering with friends or family. Invite everyone to bring their own supplies. This is a great way to combine supplies without purchasing extra and stay on budget.

FLOWER

MEDICINE

FLOWER MEDICINE

> Once more I say, you are but roots betwixt the dark sod and the moving heavens. And oftentimes have I seen you rising to dance with the light, but I have also seen you shy. All roots are shy. They have hidden their hearts so long that they know not to do with their hearts.
>
> Kahil Gibran
> The Garden of the Prophet

Simply being in presence with flowers provides a gentle remedy in the heaviest moments. In a space beyond words, flowers offer quiet medicine to deliver meaning and ease suffering.

Mindfully choosing flowers with care can deepen their healing qualities, welcoming nourishment, comfort, and renewal. Each stem holds its own unique medicine. Choosing with awareness invites you to discover the healing essence within each bloom and explore the spiritual gifts they offer.

<u>Mindful prompts to support you in choosing your flower stems</u>

- What feeling or energy are you hoping to bring forth?
- What intention are you aiming to summon?
- What message are you trying to send?
- Which flowers held special meaning for you or your loved one?
- Are there shades or colors of flowers that naturally call to you?
- Where would you like to gather your flowers?
- What kind of healing or nourishment does certain flowers offer?

FLOWER DRYING

Flowers hold wisdom in their cycles of bloom and surrender, showing us the rhythm of life and death. From seed to sprout, bud to blossom, wilt to wither, we all yield tenderly to the turning of time. Even as flowers dry out, their form mirrors a dying human body. As we die our skin shows signs of dehydration. Our vessels forage for moisture and our skin appears crepey, wrinkly, and thin. We begin to arrive in a fragile yet beautiful new form.

YOU'LL NEED

Fresh flowers, a heavy book, additional weights (e.g., extra books, a weight, a brick), scissors or garden shears.

Pressing flowers

- Select blooms that are not dry and not overly thick.

- Select a large, heavy book you'd not mind possibly staining. Option to line the page with absorbent paper (plain printer paper or parchment paper).

- Lay blooms face down spacing apart so they don't overlap and stick together.

- Close book, then stack more heavy books or objects on top to maintain pressure.

- Leave undisturbed for about 2-4 weeks.

- Store or display.

FLOWER DRYING

YOU'LL NEED

Fresh flowers, scissors or garden shears, string, twine, or rubber bands, and a dark, dry, well-ventilated space.

Hanging dry

- Choose blooms and remove excess foliage from stems to prevent mold.

- Bundle them by tying securely with string, twine, or a rubber band.

- Suspend bundle upside down in a dark, dry area with good airflow.

- Allow to dry. Drying typically takes 1-3 weeks.

Whispers through the flowers: affirmations for speaking quiet truths

I am cherished and upheld by those around me.

It is okay to take things one step at a time.

I will allow myself to rest when my body needs it.

Not everybody will understand my situation, and it is okay.

I am resilient in the face of any challenge.

I am capable of facing any challenges that come my way.

I am allowed to ask for what I need.

I can lean on others for support.

It is enough to do my best.

It's okay not to know everything.

I belong here, and I deserve to take up space.

I am grateful for this experience.

I don't have anything to prove to myself or anybody else. I am enough.

This darkness won't last forever.

The boundaries I set will protect me and my relationships.

I deserve time for myself by tending to my own needs without guilt or apology.

I'm proud of how far I have come.

flower frog

FLOWER MEDICINE

FLOWER FROG

Flower frogs help secure the stems of the flowers as you mindfully arrange the greenery in a vessel. They aid in anchoring the flower arrangement in the way you desire them to take shape. Their unique design helps the bottom of the stem access the water to stay hydrated and healthy during their life.

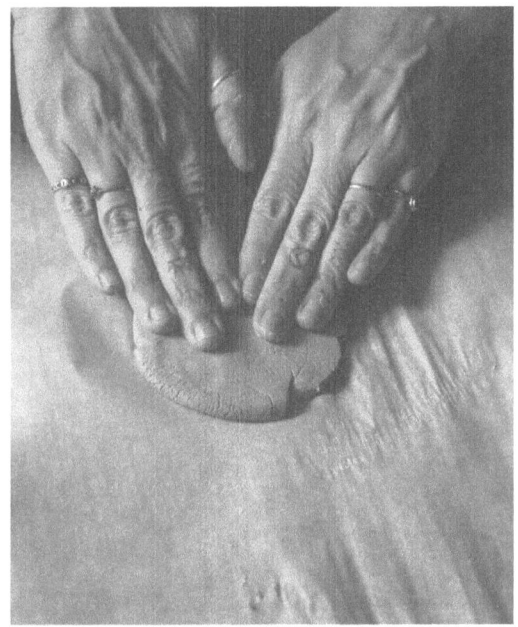

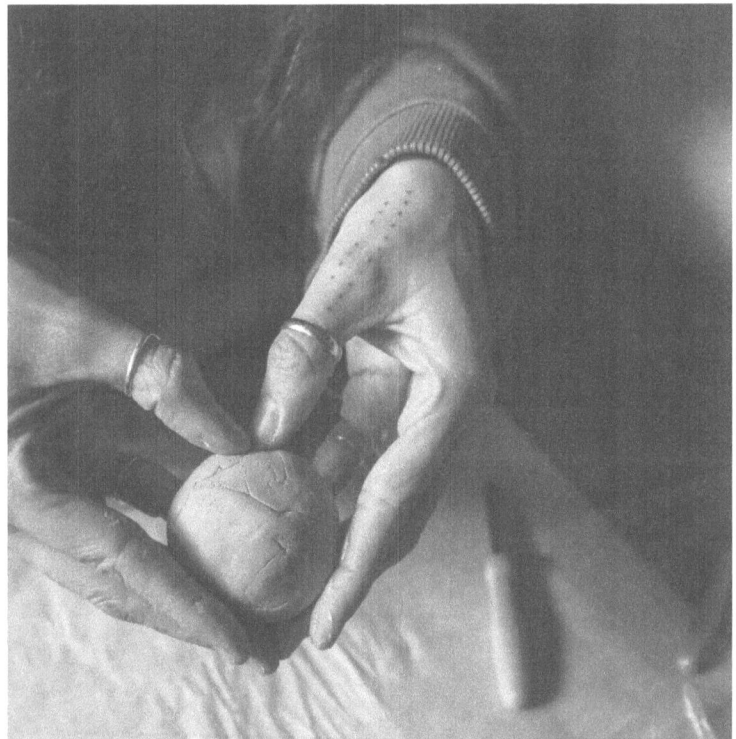

YOU'LL NEED

Air-dry clay, rolling pin or smooth glass jar (to flatten clay), jar lid to shape, a tool to poke holes for stems, small bowl of water, parchment paper, and acrylic paints (optional).

FLOWER FROG

- Take a chunk of air-dry clay and knead it in your hands until it's soft and pliable. If it feels dry, dip your fingers in water and work it in.

- Roll the clay into a ball and then gently flatten into a disk (about ¼ to ½ inch thick).

- Using a jar lid, press top into clay and tear off excess.

- Use your fingers dipped in water to smooth cracks or rough edges.

- Press and gently poke holes through the clay. Make sure the holes are wide enough for flower stems but not too big that the flowers wobble.

- Leave your clay flower frog on flat surface to air dry completely. This usually takes 24-28 hours. Flip it over halfway through to ensure even drying.

- Option to paint with acrylics or leave natural for a rustic look.

Contemplation with a flower

Begin by settling into a comfortable seat, where your body can rest with ease. Place the flower arrangement before you so they meet you eyes. Allow your gaze to rest softly upon them.

Take in the form of the flowers. Notice their size, their hues, the curve of each petal, and the leaves that surround them.

As you connect with the flowers, what presence do they radiate?

Pause and reflect if there are any feelings that stir within you. Open yourself to whatever arises.

Attend to the feelings that surface and sense where they rest within your body. Invite your breath to softly enter those spaces.

When you're ready, reach out for the flowers. Touch the blossoms with care. Let your fingers meet the tender petals.

Notice their contrast with the sharper edges of the leaves. Honor each part of their being.

Bring the flowers up your nose and breathe in their scent. Allow their essence to guide you inward. Does their fragrance call forth a memory?

Root yourself in this intimate communion with the flowers. Remain grounded in the present for as long as feels right.

medicine bottles

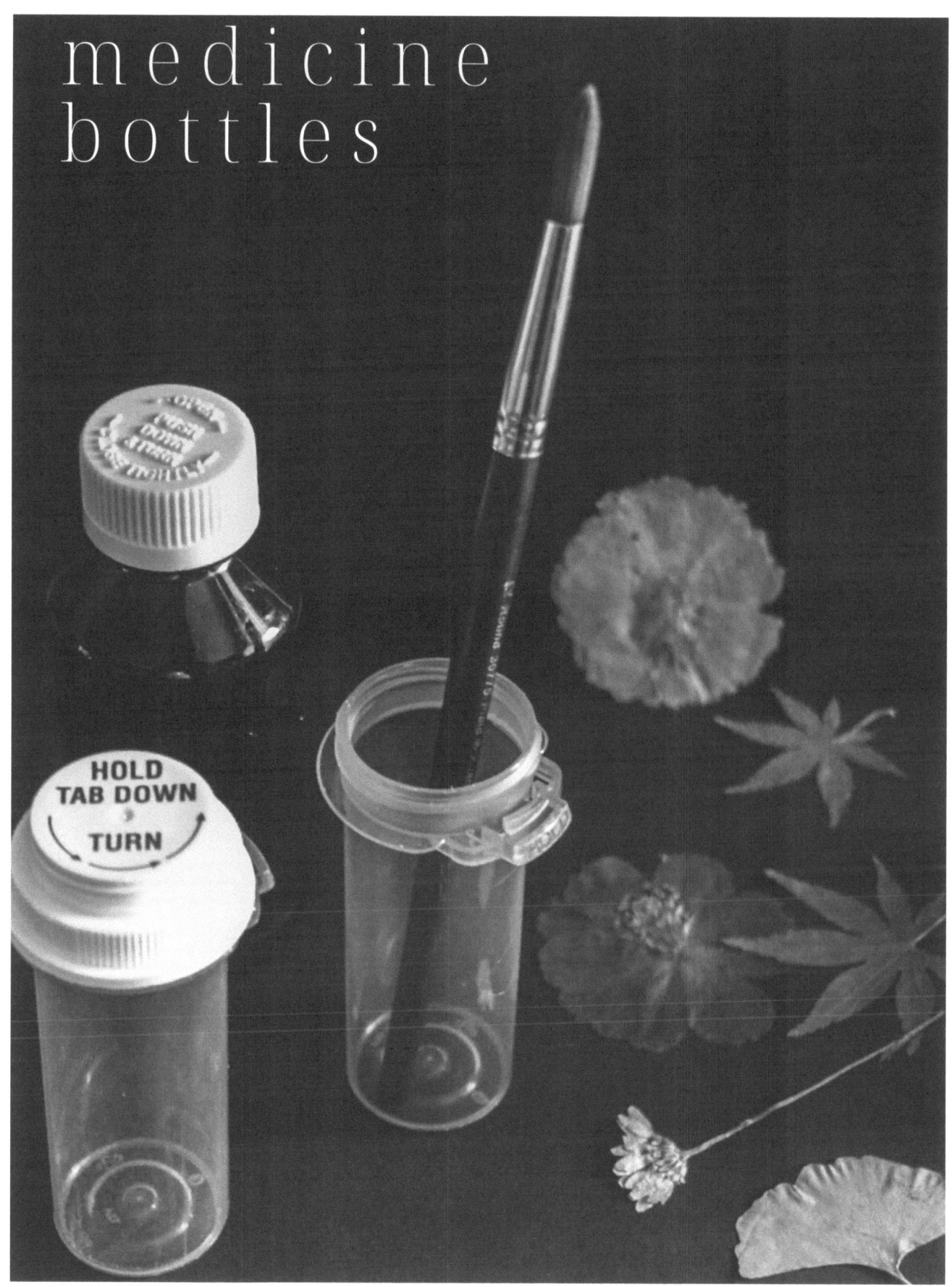

FLOWER MEDICINE

MEDICINE BOTTLES

At first glance, being in presence with multiple medications can feel overwhelming and heavy. Their sight can be a lot to take in during this tender time. Even though these bottles hold remedies meant to ease the bodies struggle, they can appear depressing, cold, and clinical.

Decorating medicine bottles can help shift the emotional experience of seeing them. The act of decorating transforms them into intentional vessels rather than impersonal containers, helping us feel more connected and in control. By visually transforming the bottles, the unsettling feelings can be softened, reclaiming the experience creating a calmer and more nurturing environment.

YOU'LL NEED

Medicine bottles (cleaned and labels removed), dried pressed flowers (see Flower Drying page 3), Mod Podge, small paintbrush, scissors or tweezers, paper towels or scrap paper (to protect your work surface).

- Prepare the bottles thoroughly, removing labels and any sticky residue. Dry completely before starting.

- Brush a thin layer of Mod Podge onto the bottle where you'll place the flowers or leaves.

- Using tweezers or your fingers, carefully place each pressed flower or leaf onto the bottle.

- Brush a thin layer of Mod Podge over the top of the flowers and leafs, covering petals and surrounding bottle area.

- Smooth out any air bubbles or wrinkles.

- Allow the bottle to dry fully before handling (usually a few hours).

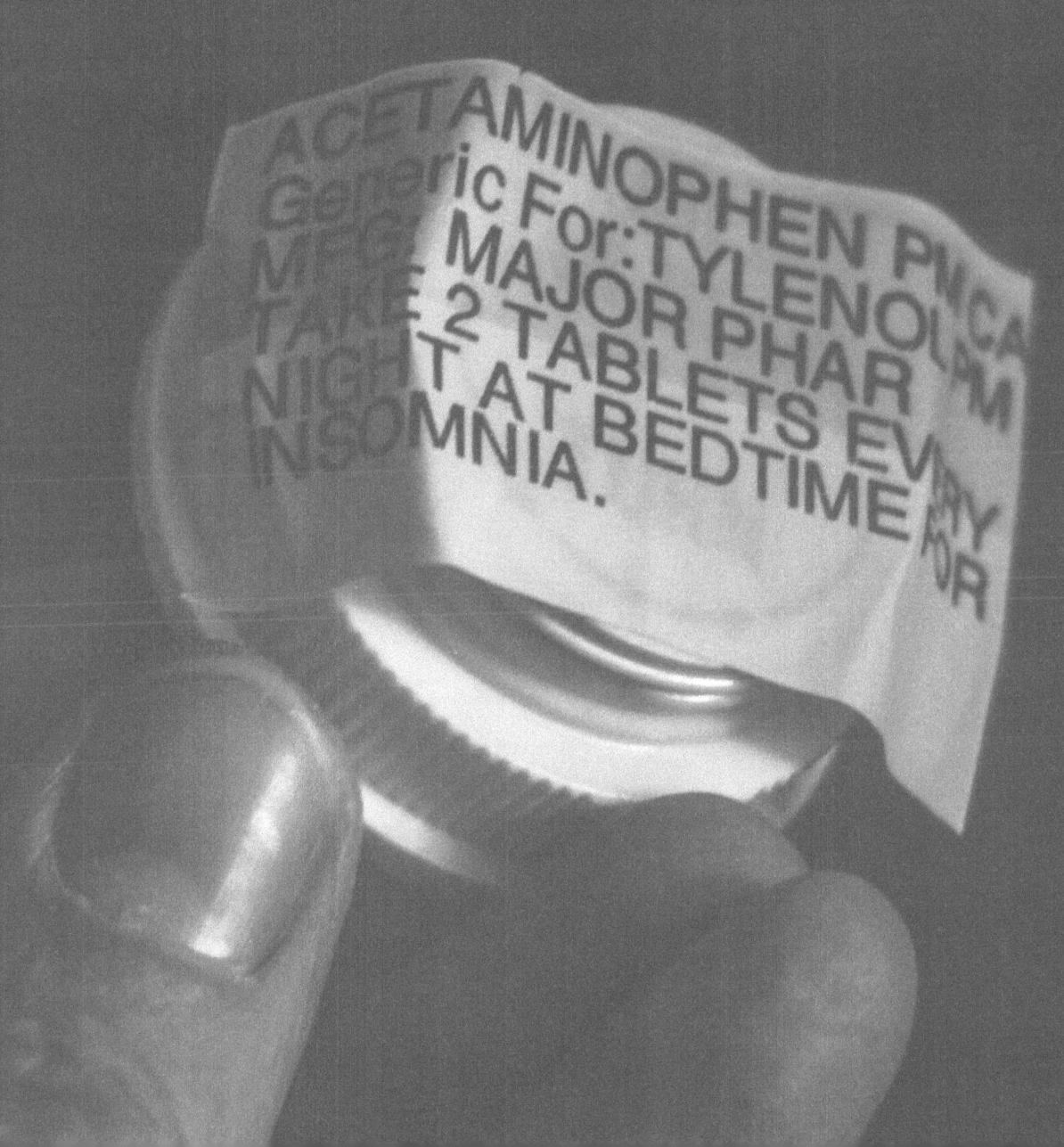

HELPING HAND

Secure a piece of the original label to the bottle cap or base so the contents are easily identifiable.

Medicine mantras

A mantra is a verbal expression or thought used to anchor and carry a chosen intention. Infusing spoken words guides thought, presence, and spirit. The following are gentle invocations to nurture peace during medicine administration. To be thought or read aloud as you administer medications to your loved one at end of life.

May this dose bring you comfort.

In this new moment, you are free to let go.

You are worthy of a good death.

You are supported, nurtured, and safe.

May you embrace stillness and inner peace.

Let every drop (or pill) release tension, struggle, and worry.

Trust in your life's unfolding.

With each dose, may you feel cared for.

You are deserving of rest.

May your body be eased and heart be soothed.

Wishing you release and surrender.

You are seen and witnessed in this moment.

Your body and spirit are honored.

You are not alone.

crown
of
love

FLOWER MEDICINE

YOU'LL NEED

Fresh flowers, foliage or greenery (eucalyptus, ferns, willow, etc.), florist wire (thin, flexible), and wire cutters or scissors.

CROWN OF LOVE

Crowns are the representation of wholeness, unity, and the eternal loop with no beginning or end. In many traditions, the deceased are adorned with flowers to signify honor, passage, and transformation.

The sacred expression of flower crowning embodies the truth that death is not an end, but a return and continuation. A crown placed over a heart gives reverence to a connection everlasting beyond death, the immortality of love.

- Choose and prepare your base stems (e.g., eucalyptus, willow). These should be longer pieces as they will be the base of the crown. Option to remove excess foliage from stems.

- Using your base stems, shape and weave into a circle. If you want more sturdiness, wrap two stems together and wire together.

- Attach flowers to the base. Starting with one flower, weave it around the crown base and secure with wire, wrapping tightly around both the stem and the base.

- Attach small springs of foliage to the base securing with wire, wrapping tightly as you go. Continue until the entire circle is covered.

- Continue working your way around the crown layering flowers and foliage, and adding extra greenery to fill gaps and soften transitions between blooms.

- Lay the crown of flowers upon your love one, blessing their body with this final adornment.

Being with the body

When someone is actively dying, we are witnessing a process already in motion. What is unfolding is not unexpected. It is the body's way of closing circle. Once final breaths have occurred there is nothing left to do but be present with your person.

May the following offerings invite final acts of reverance for your loved one and their vessel

- Wash and cleanse their body before it naturally stiffens. This can be done in the bed with a bowl of water, soap, and a wash cloth. Gently blessing their body with tender hands offers a final act of gentle care.

- Shroud or drape your loved one's body with special linens, offering a sweet embrace in their final transition.

- Lovingly adorn your loved ones with flowers, placing each bloom upon and around their body as a sacred offering.

- Sit with reverence, allowing yourself to witness and honor their final form. Embrace the natural physical changes as their body cools and settles.

- Remain in quiet presence with your loved one's body for as long as you wish. When you feel ready, you may contact the care team, who will guide the next steps quickly and smoothly.

- As the care team prepares to take your beloved's vessel, consider asking them to drape a treasured blanket over the body, easing your last viewing with warmth and tenderness. This can create a sacred and soothing space for your farewell.

Keep in mind, remaining with their body for many hours may delay or prevent organ donation from being possible. If organ donation is important, it is helpful to remember that the timing of keeping their body nearby can make a difference.

Guidelines and regulations around keeping a loved one's body at home are not the same everywhere. It is advised to look into your communities own laws and standards of care.

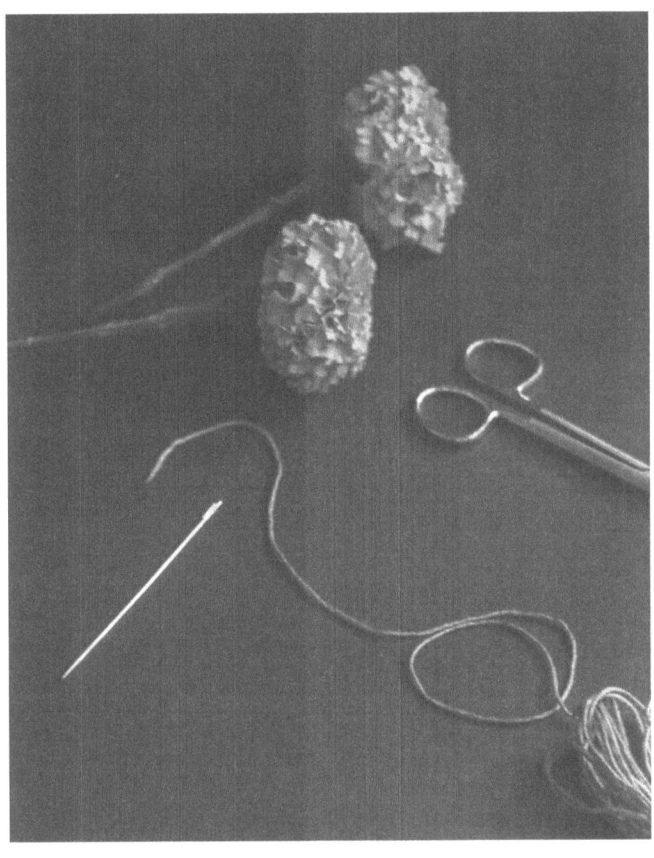

MARIGOLD GARLAND

In a season of death, marigolds hold the duality of sun and shadow. As flowers so rich in color but short lived, they embody the brilliance of being and the ache of parting. As a flower garland, they reflect devotion, remembrance, and the presence of spirit. Alongside an altar the garland becomes an honoring of the sacred and a bridge between the physical and spiritual realms.

YOU'LL NEED

Fresh marigold flowers, thread or string, a large sewing needle, and scissors.

- Cut your thread or string to desired length, leaving a few inches at the end for tying.

- Thread your needle and tie a knot at the end securely.

- Trim down the flowers leaving a short nub for sturdiness.

- Pierce the base of each marigold flower with the needle. Slide it down the string so it rests against the knot.

- Continue adding flowers one by one, gently pushing them close together.

- Once you reach the desired length, tie a secure knot at the end. Leave a few inches of string for hanging or draping around your altar or sacred space.

- Display your garland on your altar, hang it above sacred objects, or use it to adorn a photo, statue, or offering space.

Sun + shadow
a self care practice

Begin by finding the sun, where the divine light warms your skin.

Sit or stand up tall.

Sense each point of contact from your body and the ground beneath you.

Envision roots unfurling from within you, anchoring into the shadowed soil below. Each root intertwining with unseen tunnels of the earth.

Now, from rooting we rise.

Begin to elongate your spine.

Grow tall through the crown of your head, as though flowering into the light above.

Ease your shoulders downward, softening them as sunlight pours over you.

Invite the gentle heat of the sun to melt the tension from your face.

Lay a hand across your heart and another on your belly, breathing deeply into yourself.

As the sun gives way to shadow, notice the cooling breath of air upon you.

As you breathe in sense the gentle chill of air as it enters your nostrils, refreshing your whole being.

Bring both palms to meet and rub them together until warmth gathers. Lay your warmed hands over your eyes.

Sense how the warmth you create mirrors the sun, a reminder that even in shadow, light is with you.

MEMORIAL PETALS

The scattering of flower petals is an act of remembrance, reverence, and final farewell. Memorial petals, specifically a mixture of dried plant materials are often used in ceremonies like funerals or memorial services to scatter. In lieu of releasing our loved ones ashes, casting memorial petals mirrors the symbolic act of letting go and returning to nature.

YOU'LL NEED

Dried flowers and foliage, a receptacle to house petals, a bowl to mix, and a spoon or scoop.

- Dry out the flowers (see page 5).

- Once dried, pull apart petals, buds, and leaves and place into a special bowl. Mix.

- Scoop dried petals into receptacle. This could be a memorial gift bag, mini glass container, box, or tied up in a handkerchief.

- Sharing and offering memorial petals to loved ones is a way to share remembrance of our loved ones death. This is especially true if the death nest was closed to visitors or if friends and family were unable to physically be there during the final moments. These special favors gift an offering to scatter at ones own time or to house on an altar.

Elemental casting invocations

If scattering into water

Sacred Waters, hold these blessings
in your flows embrace.
Release them into your currents.
Carry them within your cleansing streams
so they travel with ease and grace.

If sent upon the wind

Holy Wind, carry these blessings on your breath.
Whisper remembrance in your breeze.
Gently sway with their memory
as it rises toward the sky.

If laying on the earth

Beloved Earth, cradle these blessings.
Shelter them in your soil.
Nurture them in stillness,
and carry them home to your depths.

If casting into fire

Great Flame, receive these blessings in your light,
and hold them in your blaze.
Burn away the sorrow,
and return love renewed
as their memory ascends.

remembrance altar

FLOWER MEDICINE

YOU'LL NEED

Foraged finds, fresh flowers, a basket or bag to collect nature's treasures.

REMEMBRANCE ALTAR

A remembrance altar is a flat lay of gathered leaves, flowers, and natural treasures collected on quiet walks through the land offered as a gesture of reverence to our grief.

Before you begin you are invited to silently walk among nature while being with your grief. Nature holds our grief by being present and bearing witness without explanation. When we walk in quietude we become attuned to our surroundings and present with our feelings. Listen to your inner voice and honor what emotions arise for you in those moments.

From what we gather, we shape a mandala of nature's gifts, an expression honoring both memory and the presence of our emotions.

- Begin walking through nature in silence, letting the land offer its gifts. Forage gently and place the natural elements that draw your attention into a bag or basket.

- When you've finished foraging, find an open space to be the base of your altar.

- Organize your materials. Flowers with flowers. Sticks with sticks.

- Begin creating. Display the pieces in a way that speaks to you. As you place down each offering recall a memory of your loved one. Infuse its taking shape with remembrance.

- Once your altar has formed, linger with its beauty and honor the sacredness of what you shaped.

Impermanence practice

Begin by sitting in quite reverence of how your remembrance altar came to bloom.

Notice what treasures drew your attention. Take in their colors, forms, and textures. Reflect on how each element has been gathered, one by one, to create a reflection of your heart in this moment of time.

It is a brief moment of perfection in the great turning of time. A one of a kind piece that will never be created the same way.

Now, over time witness the subtle changes in the piece. The leaves unfurling. The petals softening. Perhaps some elements sway softly in the breeze. Pay attention to how you feel as they shift across the surface.

What was once a moment is now becoming memory. The altar does not mourn this change. It honors it.

Allow the elements to move with ease and grace without stepping in or repair. Impermanence is not a flaw, it's a teaching. To see beauty and let it go. To hold lightly, and to release.

Let this piece be a mirror. What in your life, once fully blossomed is now fading? What must you let go of, gently, without resistance?

Sit with this truth. Grieve, if you must. Smile, if you can.

When the time feels right, release the elements back to nature.

Let them return gracefully to the earth while holding gratitude for the presence and offerings they have brought.

YOU'LL NEED

4" black ritual candle, tea-light candle, dried flower petals, and a lighter or match.

MEMENTO MORI

Memento Mori, the timeless reminder of our shared mortality, is one of the few certainties we carry in this life. Death is the path that awaits us all, yet its mystery often stirs fear. It remains the great unknown, unseen, and unspoken, in a world that has learned to turn away from its mention.

But, what unfolds when we dare to look closely at the path of death and allow light to touch it? In that illumination, we begin to see that death holds its own beauty, inviting us into presence and mindfulness. Our eyes slowly awaken, our hearts soften to the experience. Each ending in our lives deserves to be met with intimacy and reverence.

This candle serves as a beacon for death unfolding. It is a tool to honor the sacred journey coming to a close. Here, you are invited to move into the darkness. Allow the flame to light your way through the darkest hour.

- Begin by lighting your tea-light candle and setting an intention.

- Crumble, rip, or tear dried petals. Place into pile on a covered surface.

- Once the tea-light candle has formed a layer of melted wax, blow the flame out with care.

- Dip the base of the black ritual candle into the melted wax.

- While the wax is still warm, roll the bottom of the candle into the pile of petals.

- Allow to dry.

<u>Candle Safety*</u>
<u>Use caution with hot wax. Never leave lit candle unattended.</u>

Flickers of finite: a flame gazing meditation

Begin by finding a seat in a quiet, dark space. Place your candle on a stable surface. Come into stillness.

Bring awareness to your breath, taking a deep inhale through your nose and an audible exhale out through your mouth.

You have arrived.

Light your candle and whisper the following words... **remember you must die.**

Draw your attention to the flame, soften your gaze.

Witness the flame as it lives, as it moves in rhythm, and as it ascends.

Remember you must die.

When the moment feels whole, gently extinguish the candle.

As the candle goes out and the smoke lifts toward the unseen... **remember you must die.**

Remain in meditation for as long as feels right, then offer gratitude to yourself for the practice.

G R I E F

GRIEF

> The grief journey requires contemplation and turning inward. In other words, it requires depression, anxiety, and loss of control. It requires going into the wilderness.
>
> Wolfelt
> Holding Space

Grief is derived from the Latin root, grāvere, meaning to make heavy. Heaviness has always been woven into grief. From this root also gave rise to the words grave and gravity, reflecting the heaviness of sorrow.

In becoming a bearer of grief, hold close the truth that you are not alone. As feelings of loneliness arise, trust that there are others that adorn a broken heart. Your village will form. Your circle will gather. It may not be those you imagined, but often from surprising and unforeseen hearts. They'll be the ones that walk alongside you, truly see you, hear you, and affirm the fullness of your emotions.

Grief is a never ending journey. The deep-rooted sorrow will remain in our bones leaving our grief work never truly finished. Grief may reveal itself through sadness, numbness, loneliness, rage, and at times, joy. Give yourself permission to experience these feelings when they come to light. Grieving is a healthy and natural way to be with and express our feelings. Creating space to be with your grief allows our hearts to open and receive it in all of its manifestations.

mourning handkerchief

GRIEF

MOURNING HANDKERCHIEF

Hand-stitching a mourning handkerchief is both craft and ritual. Each stitch is an embodiment for our sorrow and quiet acknowledgement of our grief. The word "tears" becomes more than thread on fabric, it becomes a vessel for sorrow, a witness to loss, and a soft anchor to weep into when emotions feel overwhelming. Keep it in a pocket, place on an altar, and hold it when you need grounding in moments of sadness.

YOU'LL NEED

A plain handkerchief or cloth, embroidery hoop, embroidery floss, embroidery needle, small scissors, and water-soluble fabric pen or chalk.

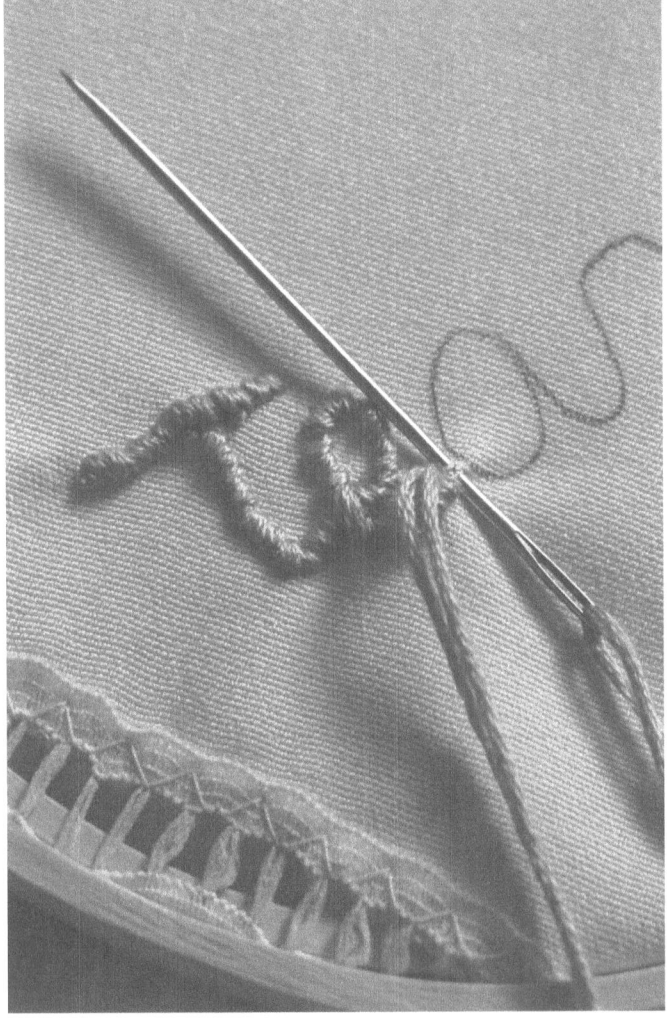

- Place the handkerchief in the embroidery hoop, smoothing it taut.

- Lightly write "tears" where you want it to rest.

- Choose a color that speaks to your grief, thread your needle, and knot the end gently.

- Begin to stitch. With each stitch, let yourself linger in thought or memory.

- As the letters form, imagine your sorrow finding a resting place here, stitched into something that can hold it for you.

- Finish with care. Tie off the thread, trim neatly, and hold the cloth in your hands.

Sitting with your tears

Settle into a place where your heart can rest, your spirit feels sheltered, and where you can be undisturbed.

You might choose to lower the lights, cocoon yourself in a blanket, or let music that speaks to your grief hold you in the background.

Sit comfortably, letting your body rest with ease. Close your eyes or soften your gaze.

As your breath moves gently in and out, allow yourself to notice what feelings arise within.

Rest in stillness, where absence of doing makes room for grief to find its voice and emotions can surface to be felt fully.

Empower yourself to surrender to your sadness. Should tears arise, receive them. Do not push them away or suppress them.

Receive the tear upon your cheek as a tiny messenger, carrying healing in its path. Allow its presence to soften what aches inside. Trust that your tears know what needs to be spoken without words.

Perhaps you allow yourself to unravel into sobs that shake the body, a cry raw and unshaped, carrying the ancient sound of sorrow that longs to be heard.

Dwell in the honesty of your sorrow. Allow its currents to stir and depart. Hold yourself here for some time.

Receive what emerged, and meet it with tenderness.

When the moment feels right, soften your mind into your heart. Give thanks for the truth of your tears and the love they reveal.

grief tree

GRIEF

YOU'LL NEED

Pressed dried leaves (see Flower Drying page 3), small branches or twigs, paint pens, hole punch, a simple tie (string, yarn, or twine), and a vase or vessel.

GRIEF TREE

A grief tree holds your vulnerable sorrow in the open, where it can breathe. An artwork where pressed leaves become the canvas for the grief you carry. Each word, drawn in paint, rests on fragile veins and branches, becoming a reminder to not hide but to let yourself be seen.

- Dry out and press leaves (see page 3).

- Using a paint pen, write words, phrases, or even single emotions on the leaves.

- Use a hole punch to create a hole in the leaf and secure with string. Handle carefully; they are delicate, just like the emotions they carry.

- Hang and arrange your inscribed leaves onto the branches in a way that feels meaningful. Let your intuition guide you.

- Display your piece somewhere you can see it. Let it be a daily reminder that your grief has a place. Your feelings do not need to be hidden.

Seasons of grief

As life cycles through seasons, grief, too, unfolds in its own seasonal passage. Mourning weathers its own seasons. Our inner seasons of grief may not always align with the seasons outside. Grief keeps its own calendar. For example, grief may be in winter in the height of natures summer, or spring in the depth of autumn. Grief asks to be tended to in its own time, regardless of the season unfolding beyond us. What matters is that we honor the season within, even when it does not match the season without.

Blessings for the seasons of grief

Fall

As I step into the season of fading light,
I slowly shed grief, leaf by leaf.
I allow my sorrow to fall like leaves
nourishing the soil beneath.

Winter

May I settle into a time of rest
where the cold carries a heavy silence.
I embrace the stillness of cocooning within my grief
in a season waiting for lights return.

Spring

As I emerge into the season of both ache and awakening
may my tears soften the ground where my sorrow is planted.
Let the waters nourish the soil of my grief,
and allow a tender flowering like blooms in spring.

Summer

As I move into long days stretched by longing
let my sorrows be bathed in sunlight.
I allow the heat of the season
to kindle the embers within my mourning.

shatter and release

GRIEF

SHATTER AND RELEASE

This practice turns an ordinary plate into a sacred vessel for release. On its surface, you write the grief, anger, or burdens that feel too heavy to carry. When the plate is shattered, the sound and fragments become a symbolic letting go, a breaking open that clears space for healing.

Write it down. Let it go.

YOU'LL NEED

A ceramic plate (thrifted or inexpensive), permanent markers, a safe space for breaking outdoors, protective gear (safety glasses, gloves), and a strong bag to contain shards.

- Find a quiet space. Take your plate and marker, and pause to reflect on what you're holding onto (grief, anger, fear, regret).

- On the surface of the plate, write words, phrases, or symbols that represent the feelings, memories, or burdens you want to release.

- Place the plate in a strong bag and tie ends shut. Find an open space outdoors then drop, let go, or throw it to the ground. Let the breaking be your act of release.

- Witness the pieces. Look at the shards. Notice the beauty in the brokenness, the sharp edges that once held heavy words.

- Collect the pieces and discard them as a gesture of letting go.

Grief support

It takes a village to care for the dying, the caregiver, and the grieving. This path is not meant to be done alone.

It is important to find your community. Surrounding yourself with others who have experienced similar losses can offer care, understanding, and give reassurance that you are not alone in your journey.

<u>If you are seeking ways to support someone in grief</u>

- Listen actively without judgement.

- Offer a shoulder to cry on.

- Validate their feelings.

- Simply show up and share space.

- Talk about their loved one and share memories.

- Offer an embrace, hug, or a hand hold if they are open to it.

- Respect their grieving process.

- Avoid giving unsolicited advice.

- Offer support with daily tasks.

- Let them know you are there for them and care about them.

- Continue to check in. Grief lasts a lifetime.

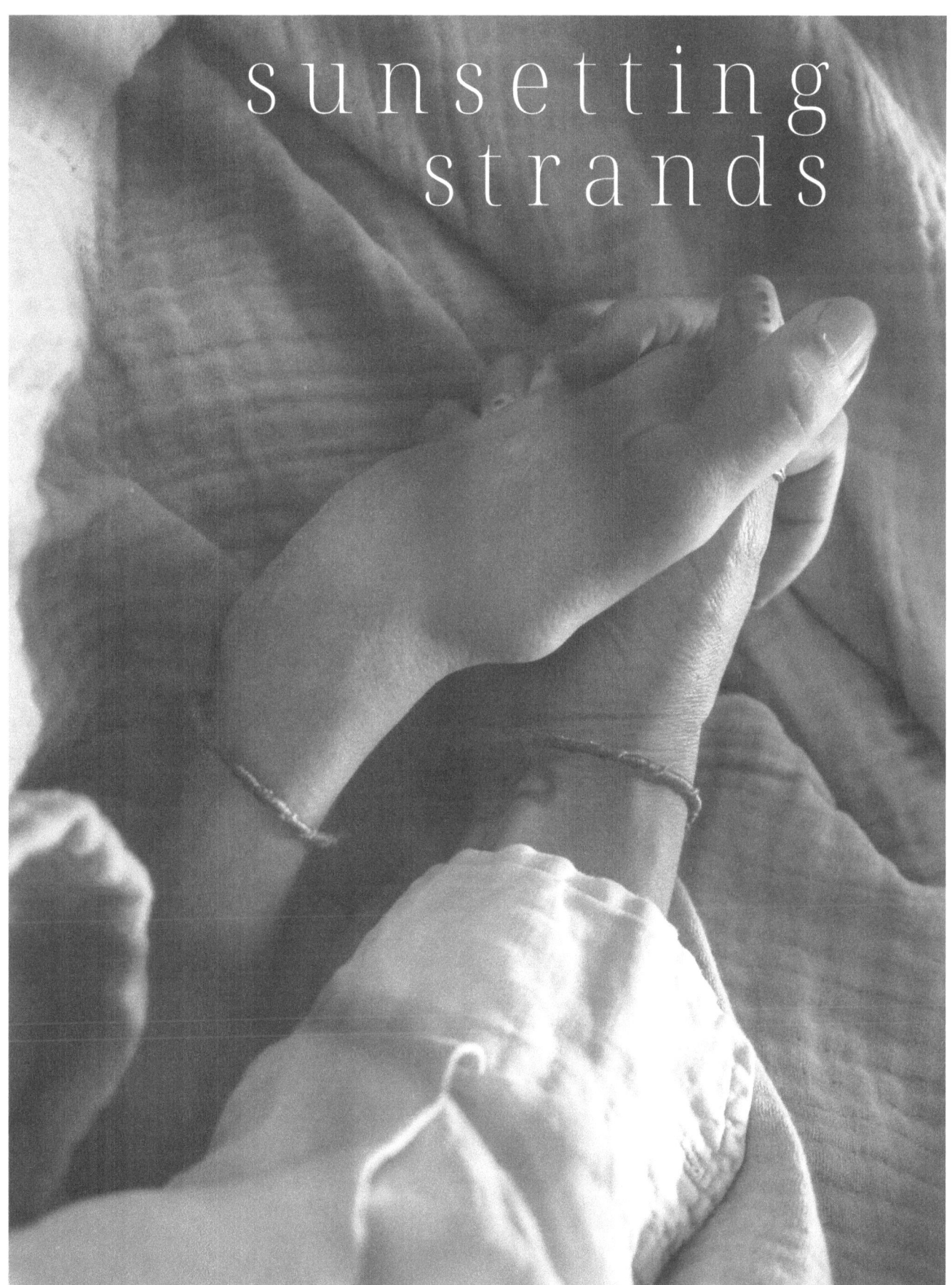

sunsetting strands

GRIEF

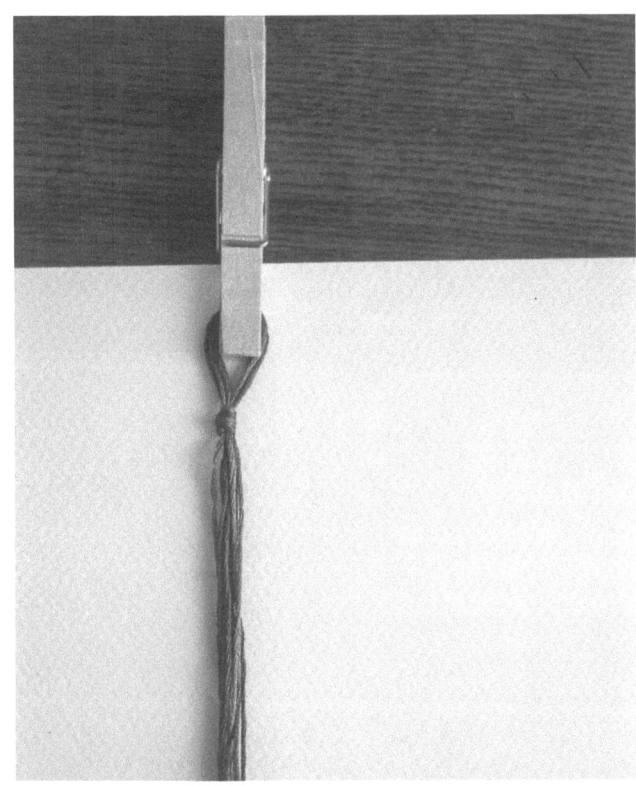

SUNSETTING STRANDS

To sunset a phase in relationship is to gently release one chapter and step into another. Though the physical bond may shift or end, a new form of connection is ready to emerge. Sunsetting strands serve as a symbol of walking this threshold together. These bracelets serve as symbols of lasting companionship, tied on in love, and left to remain until they fall away on their own. Traditionally, these bracelets are fastened around a friend's wrist or ankle while holding an intention or wish in heart.

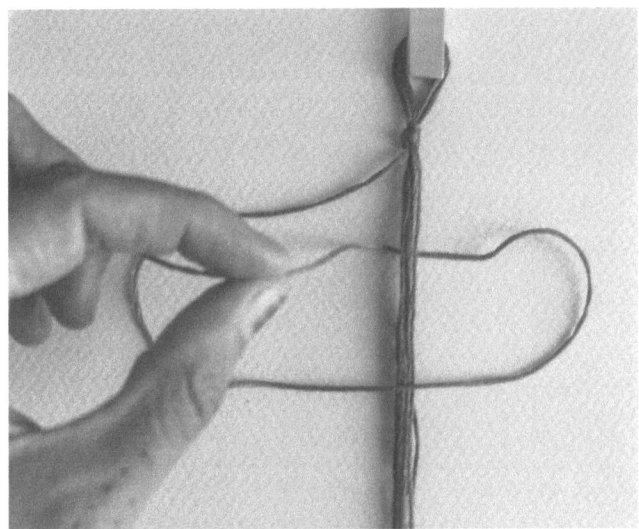

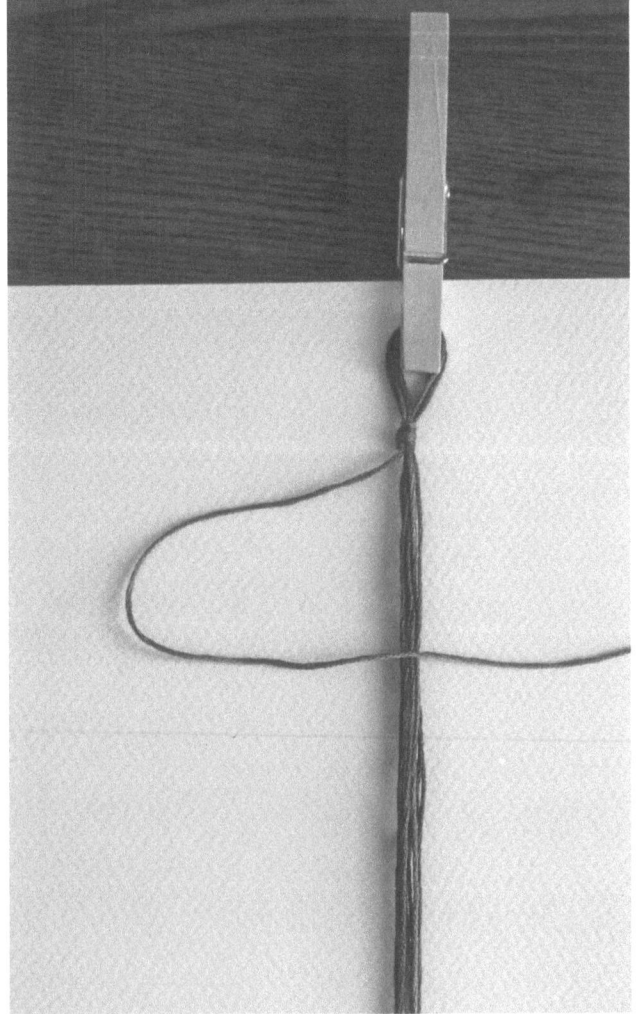

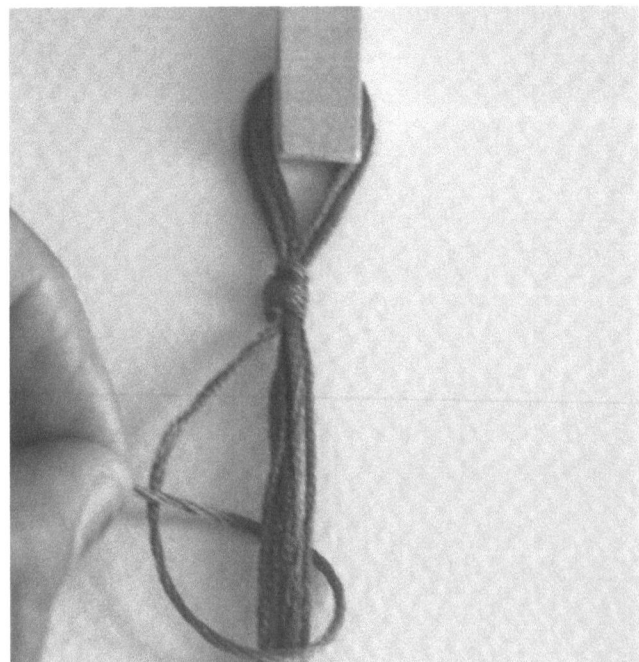

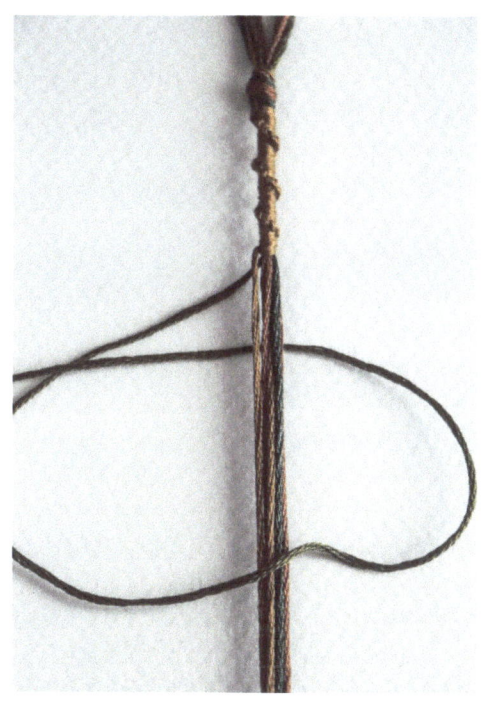

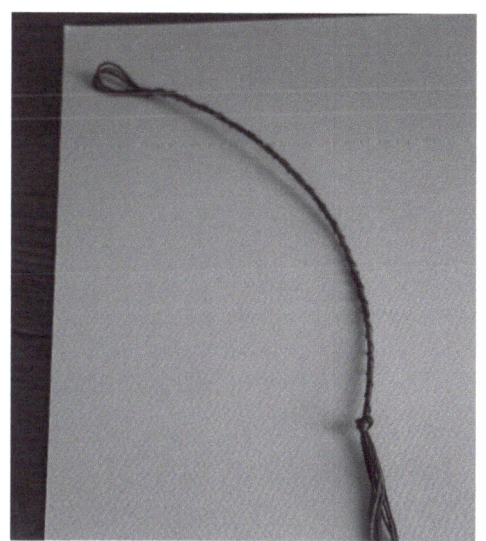

YOU'LL NEED

2-6 colors of embroidery thread (the more colors, the wider the bracelet), scissors, clothing pin, and a firm surface to hold the bracelet in place while you work (e.g., card stock, cardboard, or a clipboard).

- You'll need several strands of embroidery thread. Cut to about 45 inches long (better a little too long than too short). Gather, fold, and tie an overhead knot.

- Use a clothespin to secure the top knot onto a sturdy surface such as card stock, cardboard, or a clipboard.

- Start with the far-left string (your working string). Cross it over the strings to its right, making a number "4" shape.

- Bring the working string under the right strings and then pull up through the loop of the "4" shape.

- Pull the working string snug, sliding the knot up to your starting point, while keeping the base strands straight.

- Repeat the same step again on the same string. The knotting will begin to swirl and twist naturally. Lean into that flow.

- To switch colors, place the old working string into the center and pull a new working string to the left. The old color is now out of the way, and the new color is ready to become the leading string.

- When it is at your desired length add a knot to the end and trim edges. Leave a 2-3 inch tail for tying on.

Unfeigned feelings: writing exercise

Writing can take several forms within a therapeutic setting. Free writing, is a form of journaling where the only instruction is to write what is on your mind. Without censoring, editing, or need of explanation describe how you feel about your loved one dying. Express how your relationship has changed or is changing. Leave it all on paper. Ignore spelling, punctuation, and penmanship. Take 2-5 minutes to move your pen. No one needs to read this and it doesn't have to be read aloud. Without judgment, narrate your honest emotions.

Example

Afraid of being alone / I hate that you're dying / We didn't get enough time / I regret not being there for you in the past / You deserved better / I hate that you were in an accident / I hate this disease / I'm scared you'll take your last breath without me in the room / I'm afraid that you'll be in pain / I wish I knew what you were thinking / Do you think I'm doing a good job taking care of you / I'm trying my best / I'm trying really really hard / This is really hard / I just want you to swallow / I want to nourish you / Will it be scary? / Are you afraid? / I'm nervous for what you'll look like / Im sad that you're losing weight / I miss your old face / I miss when you would smile / I miss hearing your voice / I'm sad more family and friends have not come to see you / I'm afraid of what happens when you're body is taken away / Will we get enough time? / I wish we had more time / You deserved better / You deserved more / We deserved more / I don't know what I will do without you / I don't know who I will be without you / Where will you go? / Will I still feel you?

GRIEF

YOU'LL NEED

Fabric, thread, and sewing needle. Optional embellishments (eg., beads, charms, elastic).

MOURNING BAND

A mourning band is traditionally a piece of black fabric, most often worn on the upper arm representing grief or loss. Typically adorned after the death of someone close, it becomes a visible symbol of mourning.

A mourning band is a personal and tender craft project, turning grief into a tangible act of remembrance and healing. When created intentionally it becomes more than a symbol of loss, it becomes a woven expression of memory, love, and transition. Making one by hand invites you into a quiet, mindful space where grief can move through your body, breath, and fingertips.

Using fabric that holds meaning, perhaps a piece of clothing from a loved one or a color that evokes their essence, you can create a physical representation of your connection. Adorning it with charms, beads, or stitching can make it uniquely yours. As you fold, cut, stitch, or tie you may find your sorrow softening. It is a way to carry what you have lost with intention. Genuinely, wear your broken heart on your sleeve.

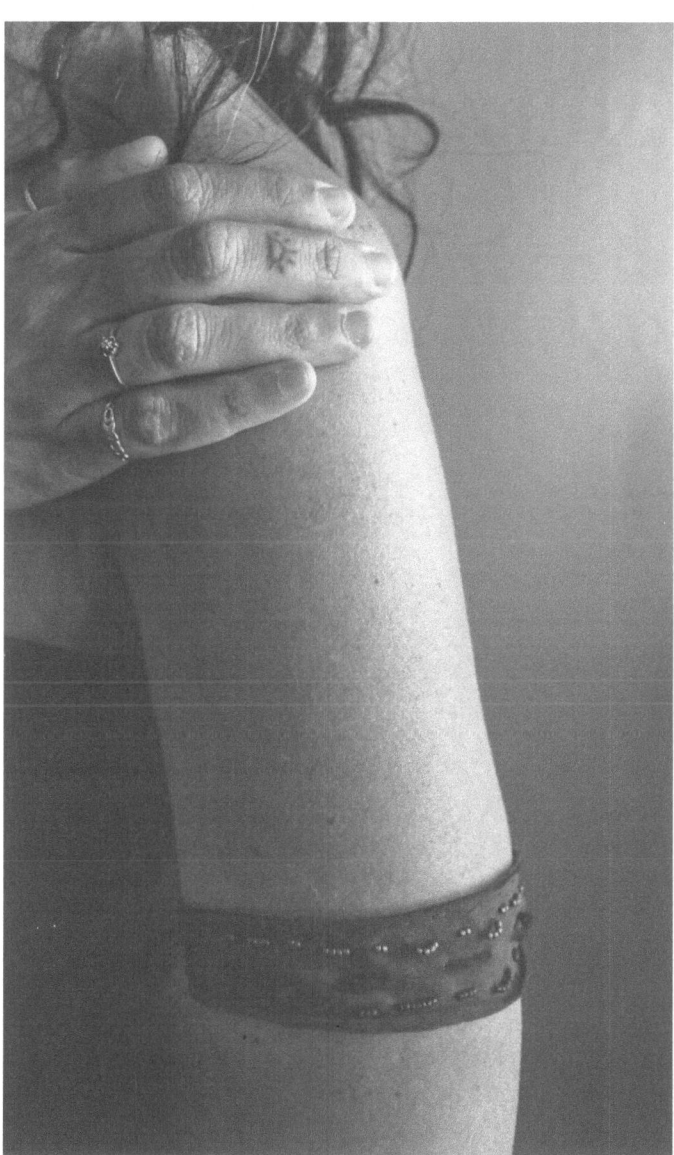

- Choose your fabric intentionally. You might repurpose something that carries memory (a shirt, pillowcase, or scarf).

- Cut a strip long enough to wrap around your upper arm. Standard width is 2-3 inches, but follow your intuition.

- Sew and hem the edges (optional) for a clean edge, or leave raw to reflect the unraveling that grief brings.

- Add meaningful touches. Embroider initials, birth / death dates, or perhaps add charms, beads, or buttons from their favorite coat.

- Decide how you would like to close the piece. Option to add elastic on the inside and sew the edges together. A simpler option is to wrap the fabric and secure with a simple knot.

Band of anchors

An anchor is something that steadies you when life feels unsteady. It helps you return to yourself, to the present moment, and to a sense of calm. It's a way of gently tethering back to what is real and grounding. Here are a few anchoring techniques that have supported me personally.

Breathwork
Take a few slow, steady breaths. Inhale gently through your nose to a count of four. Exhale softly through your mouth to a count of four. Continue this rhythm for several rounds, allowing each breath to ease you into calmness.

If it feels supportive, you might let your exhale carry sound, an audible breath that helps release tension. This might take form of a sigh, a low growl, or even a full-bodied scream.

Earthing
Wherever you find yourself, pause for a moment. Slip off your shoes and let your bare feet rest on the ground. Notice the earth holding you, the soil beneath drawing you gently back into the here and now.

Safe space
Seek out a place where you feel safe and at ease. Choose a spot that helps steady you and invites calm. For instance, you might sit by a river and place your feet in the water, letting its coolness soothe your body and settle your spirit.

Tapping
Begin with light, gentle tapping on your sternum. Notice the rise and fall of your chest, a reminder of being alive. Allow each touch to guide you back into the present moment.

Affirmations
Offer yourself gentle reminders to re-center yourself. For example:
I am safe. I am here. I can be here now. I am ok. I can trust this moment.

Name it
Give words to the emotion and to what set it in motion. For instance, I notice I am spiraling because fear is present. What's overwhelming me is fear tied to the possibility of losing my loved one all over again.

grief stones

GRIEF.

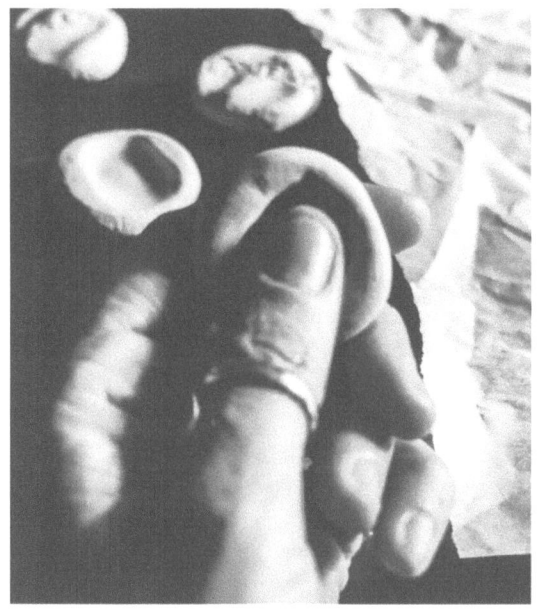

GRIEF STONES

Shaping a grief stone is a way to press your sorrow into clay, giving form to what feels formless inside. The act itself offers a tender moment to explore how grief lives in your body. When the stone has dried, you can cradle it in your palm, letting your thumb rest and circle at its center. This simple gesture invites your awareness to settle into your grief, meeting it with presence and care. Give yourself permission to fully feel.

YOU'LL NEED

Air-dry clay, metal letter stamps (or any stamp you'd like to use), a small bowl of water, and a flat surface covered with parchment paper or wax paper.

- Break off a piece of air-dry clay that feels comfortable in your palm. Roll it between your hands until it softens, then shape it into a smooth oval or round stone.

- Press your grief into form. As you mold the clay, imagine transferring the weight of grief into its surface. Let your thumb leave a gentle impression if you'd like.

- Choose a word, name, or feeling that holds your sorrow. Use the metal letter stamps to imprint the clay on the side opposite of the thumbprint.

- If cracks appear, dip your finger in water and smooth them away. Trust the texture that emerges. Every mark can hold meaning.

- Place your stamped clay stone on parchment or wax paper and allow to dry fully (usually 24-48 hours).

- Once hardened, the stone becomes a companion you can hold in moments of remembrance.

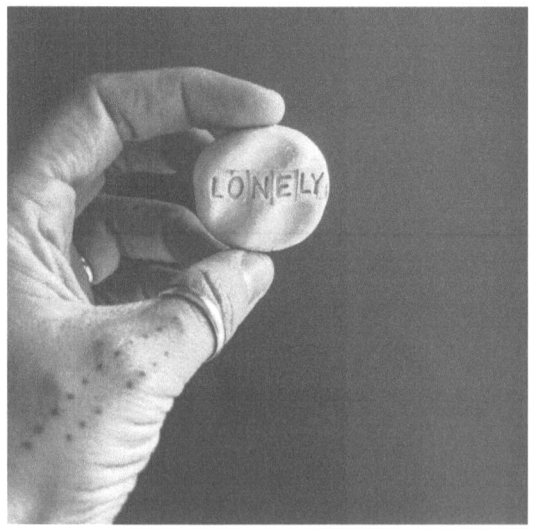

Sounding breathwork for primal grief

Choose a space where you can give yourself permission to be alone and undisturbed.

Find an upright, comfortable seat. A cushion or folded blanket can offer added support.

Holding your grief stone in your hand, gently press your thumb into its belly. Begin rubbing your thumb in a circular motion. Allow the motion against the stone to gently call up the grief that rests within you.

Guide your attention to your breathing. Allow your breath to deepen and slow. Follow your breath all the way in and all the way out. Draw in a long, slow breath through your nose followed with a deep exhale out through your mouth. Breathe in for a count of 4…3…2…1… Exhale 4…3…2…1…

Let's deepen the practice by breathing in fully and releasing with a sounding breath. As you exhale begin to engage the back of your throat and breath out in a way that would cloud up a mirror 4…3…2…1… Breathe in through the nose, and exhale as if you're fogging up a mirror. Repeat 2-4 times.

Now, expand this moment by inhaling through your nose 5…4…3…2…1… On your out-breath, allow a deep, resonant tone to emerge, similar to a moan or a sigh. 5…4…3…2…1… (2-4X)

Take a deep breath in through your nose 6…5…4…3…2…1… Now, move the sigh into your heart space, big breath out howling even louder this time 6…5…4…3…2…1… (2-4X)

Take a deep breath in through your nose 7…6…5…4…3…2…1… Including your belly this time, guttural cry out through your exhale 7…6…5…4…3…2…1… (2-4X)

Continue these primal breaths for as long as you need. You can go from silence to screaming.

When you feel finished, slowly allow yourself to let go of any forced breath and come back to your natural state of breathing. Linger here for a few breaths before returning to the rhythm of daily life.

WORDS OF WOE

Grief often lives within us without form. It is an ache in the body, a heaviness in the chest, or a silence that feels impossible to describe. By giving grief an image, we allow it to step out from the shadows and be witnessed.

This practice invites you to honor your sorrow by layering words onto a photo of yourself or a loved one. In doing so, you create a portrait that speaks the unspeakable. Grief is now able to be seen, named, and shared in a tender way.

YOU'LL NEED

A printed photo of yourself or a loved one, magazines, newspapers, printed pages with words or phrases, scissors, and glue or tape. Optional: markers, paint, or pens for additional words.

- Choose an image that feels right to work with. This might be a photo of you in this season, or of someone who is no longer here.

- Find your words. Flip through magazines or printed pages. Notice any words, or phrases that reflect your grief. Cut them out without overthinking.

- Place the words around and upon the photo. Let the arrangement be intuitive.

- Once the placement feels true, glue or tape the words down. Allow the collage to hold both clarity and messiness, just as grief does.

- Sit with the finished collage. Notice what story it tells about your grief.

- If it feels supportive, share your collage with someone you trust, allowing them to witness the shape your grief made visible.

Tending through naming

Take a moment to arrive where you are. Soften your shoulders and draw your attention inward.

Notice the rise and fall of your breath, steady and natural.

As you breathe, you are invited into the practice of naming what arises. Grief and emotion ebb and flow, sometimes hard to name.

Without judgement, begin to call your emotions by name. There is no right or wrong way to name what is here. This is not about fixing or changing. It is about witnessing your truth in this moment.

As you inhale say to yourself, *I feel …*

As you exhale (*name your emotion*).

Whatever words come to mind, allow them to come, without editing or explaining. When a word arises, hold it gently. Let it be seen. Let it be honored.

And if no words come, simply say *I am here, and something is moving within me*. That too is naming. That too is enough.

Pause here. Notice what shifts when your feelings are named. Notice how your body responds. Perhaps you feel a softening, a moment of ease, or the warmth of recognition.

When you feel ready, open your eyes, carrying with you the truth that your feelings, once spoken, become more bearable, more human, more whole.

grief garden

GRIEF

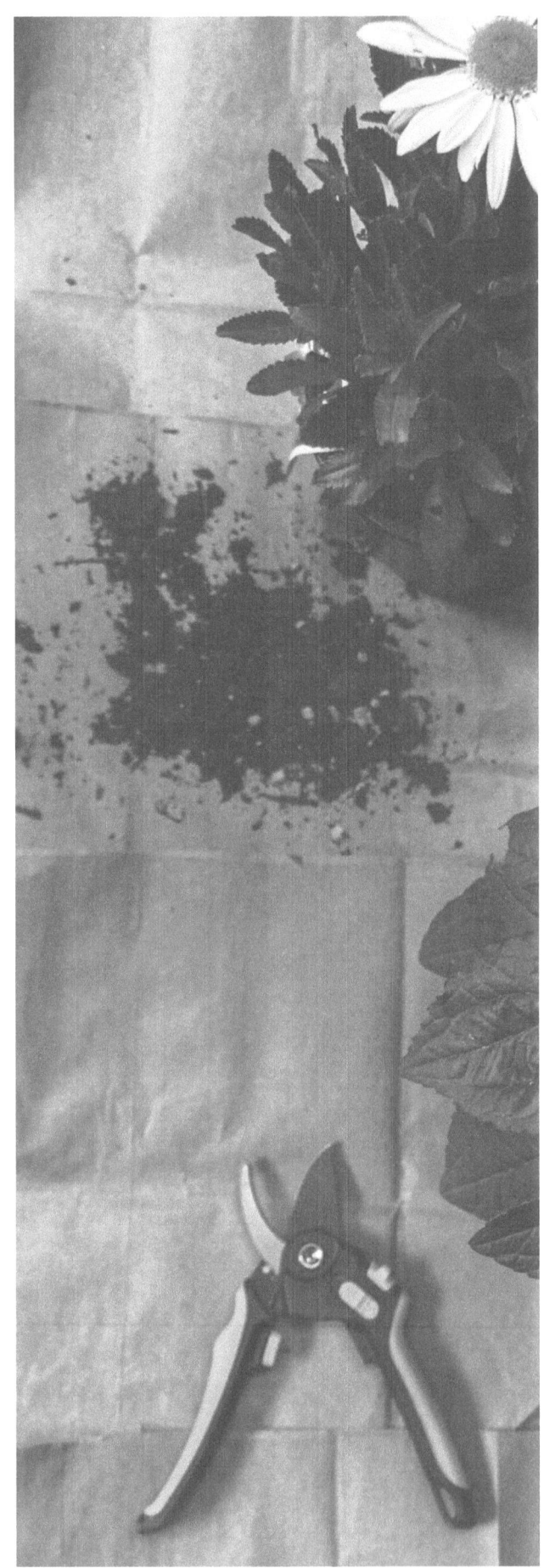

GRIEF GARDEN

When sorrow feels untethered, a garden grounds you. Tending a grief garden can steady you, even in the midst of grief. Your hands in the soil become a root, an anchoring in the weight of loss. You allow yourself to be grounded in your sadness. Each seed you nurture and every bloom unfolding becomes a living reminder of a love that never leaves.

YOU'LL NEED

Seeds or small plants, soil and a pot or a prepared patch of earth, a glass of water (for you) and a watering can.

- Dedicate an area for your grief garden. This can be indoors or outdoors.

- Pick a seed or plant with meaning and that feels right.

- Plant with intention. Dig a small hole and lay the seed or seedling in the soil. Perhaps you quietly speak "I plant this for (name / feeling). May this grow with my love."

- As you water lightly, imagine your grief being held by the earth and the love beneath continuing to nourish life.

- Sit quietly with your hands resting on the pot or soil. Allow yourself to be present and honor any feelings that arise.

- Tend and return. Water gently as the plant needs. Each visit is tending of both plant and memory.

Soil + soul

Choose a space to settle in and come to a position of comfort. Perhaps this space is outdoors or low to the ground, where you can sense the nearness of the earth beneath you.

Bring awareness to your breath, soften, and settle in.

Sense the connection between your body and the ground beneath you.

Visualize you are in an open ground and the sun is warming your skin. Maybe you are in a meadow of untamed wildflowers, a lush forest canopy, or by the waters edge.

Notice all the points of contact between your body and the earth beneath you, where the soil can support, cradle, and hold you.

Imagine tiny roots growing from where your body and the ground meet. The roots weave their way down to earth's center. The roots become stronger the farther they grow, and connect to the heart of the earth.

Become aware of the sounds around you, without judgement. Perhaps you hear the gentle whispers of the trees, a low hum in the air, or the call of a bird overhead. Listen with care, nature often carries messages of guidance if you are willing to hear them.

Notice any thoughts or feelings that come to mind. Honor each thought and envision them as if they are feathers floating in the wind.

Let yourself be present here for a while.

Breathe with ease. With each inhale gather a sense of peace. With each breath out, release and let go...

When you're ready, ease yourself back into your surroundings. Take your time as you move from the space back into the world around you.

PRAYERS

PRAYERS

Death becomes simply the final stage of my sadhana. My death... my death...

Ram Dass
Walking Each Other Home

At its essence, prayer is the practice of offering focused intention, hope, and loving energy where it is most needed. It's an internal act of love that may appear as silent reflection, quiet presence, or a heartfelt wish of peace and strength. Prayer is simply an act of the heart, open to anyone. You don't need to consider yourself religious or spiritual. With prayer, even the simplest space becomes holy.

Below are tender expressions of prayer or prayerful presence for those nearing death and their loved ones

- Holding their hand or gently touching their arm or shoulder.

- Holding someone in loving awareness.

- Sending mental or heartfelt wishes for peace, strength, and comfort.

- Being present with them in spirit.

- Remembering someone tenderly.

- Placing a hand over your heart to silently send love toward them.

- Lighting a candle.

prayer beads

PRAYERS

PRAYER BEADS

A string of prayer beads function as both art and spiritual tool. This form of beadwork provides meditative focus, allowing the user to keep track of repeated prayers or intentions. It acts as an anchor, guiding us gently into the here and now. Whether we use it for meditation or simply hold our talisman, we open ourselves to its soothing, centering, and healing presence.

YOU'LL NEED

6mm-8mm beads (let your intuition guide how many beads you include), knotting cord (size depended on bead hole size), scissors, and super glue.

- Begin by setting an intention for your piece. What energy should it carry? What emotions or comfort would you like it to offer the recipient?

- Cut a length of cord about 3-4 times the intended finished length of prayer beads.

- Dip just the tip of the cord into a small amount of super glue to form a stiff, pointed "needle." Allow the glue to dry completely and trim so it can pass through bead holes without fraying. Test the tip. If it is still flexible or becomes frayed, repeat the process with a little more glue.

- String your first bead, letting it carry the energy of your intention.

- Tie a small knot between each bead. Use a simple overhand knot and slide it snugly against each bead. *If you choose to forego the knotting process you can add a small spacer bead after each bead instead or simply allow the beads to rest together.

- As your piece grows bead by bead, knot by knot, allow it to become a vessel of your love and energy you wish to share.

- When your piece is complete, secure the ends with a knot, optionally reinforcing it with glue, and trim off any excess.

Holding prayer: gentle guidance with beads

Settle into a tall seat with your prayer beads resting in your hands.

Soften into each inhale and exhale.

Feel the presence of the beads in your palms. Sense their heaviness, texture, and temperature.

Become aware of how your body and spirit respond to their touch.

Hold close the intention that calls to you now. Perhaps peace, love, or healing.

Touch the first bead in your fingers. Hold it softly as you speak your intention silently or out loud. Allow your prayer to infuse your practice and feel how it moves through your body.

Slowly move through bead by bead. With each bead, repeat your prayer, intention, or phrase.

If words don't come to mind, simply breathe and sit in presence. Let the rhythm of moving from bead to bead be your prayer.

Continue all the way around your talisman. When you reach the final bead, close your eyes and place the strand between your hands over your heart.

Allow yourself to rest in the stillness you created.

Notice how you feel after this practice. Embrace this moment.

Offer gratitude for this moment of connection.

Know that you can return to your beads at any time.

protection bracelet

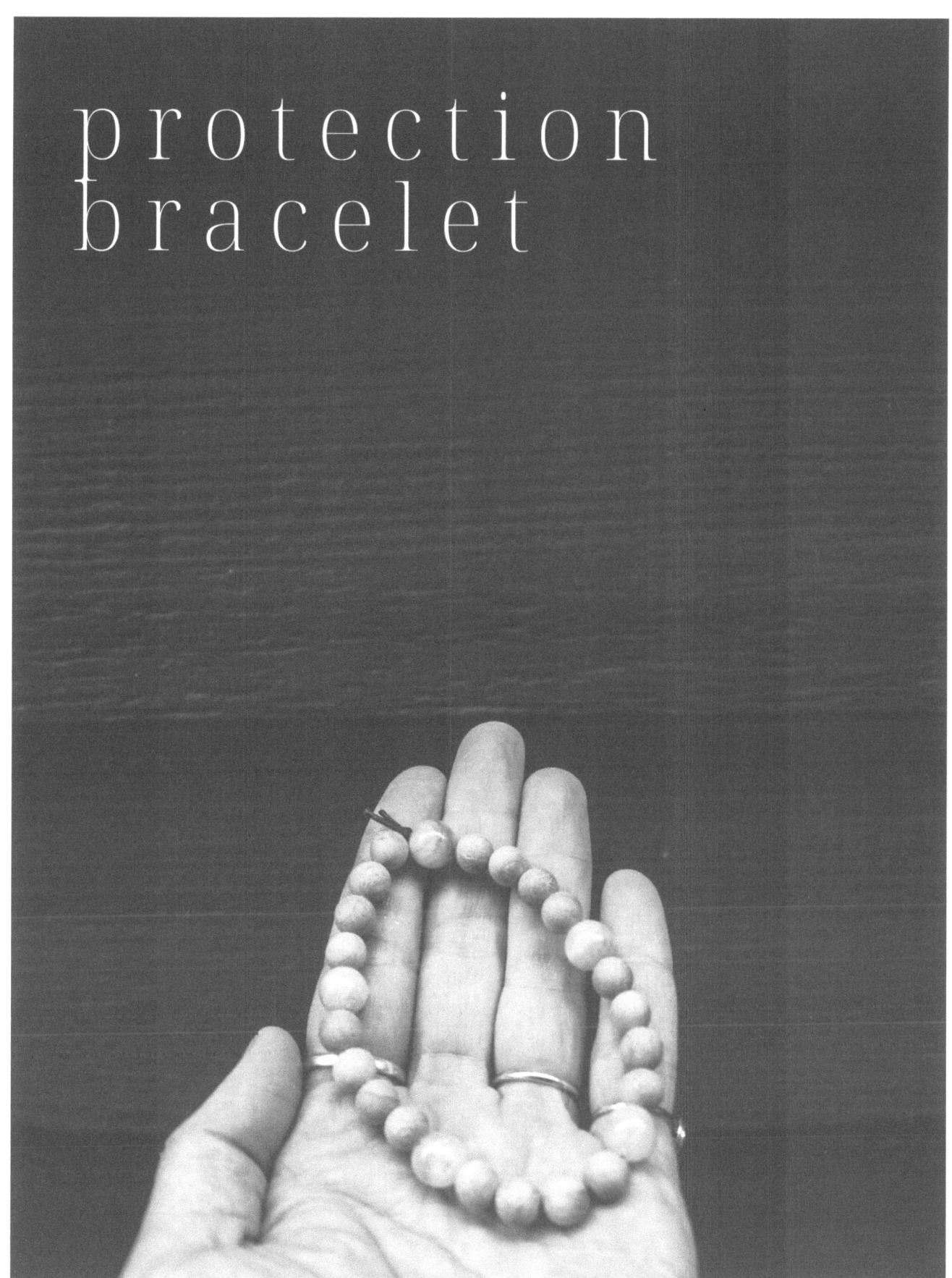

PRAYERS

YOU'LL NEED

Beads, elastic cording (0.5-1MM depending on bead hole size), scissors, and super glue (optional for securing the knot).

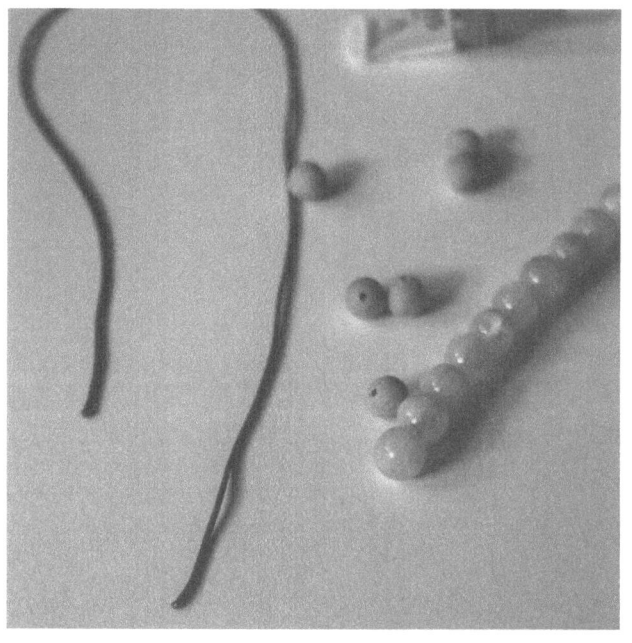

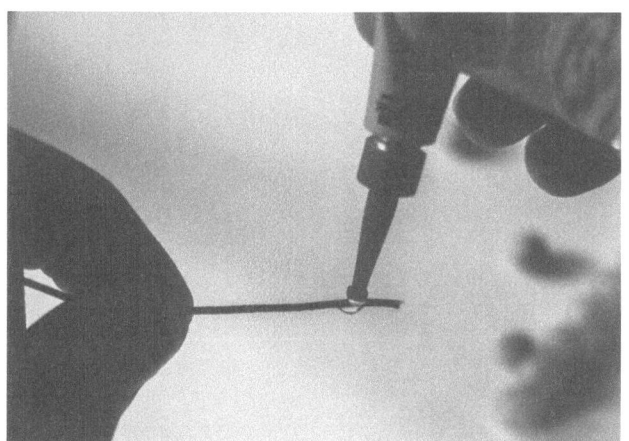

PROTECTION BRACELET

A protection bracelet is a sacred charm worn on the wrist. It serves as a guardian for the one who wears it, symbolizing comfort, support, and a shield of safety. The beads you select shape the energy of the bracelet. Let your inner wisdom and intuition guide you in choosing the energy this bracelet will carry. With each bead strung, it becomes a vessel for intention and blessing.

- Wrap the elastic cord loosely around your wrist to find the right length. Add about 4-6 extra inches to make knotting easier, then cut.

- Tie a knot at one end of your elastic string. This will help the beads stay on your cord and not slip off.

- Option to add a strip of super glue to the other end of your cord. Allow to dry. Once dried trim off the tip of the needle-like end. This will make it easier to thread on the beads.

- String your beads in any pattern or design you like. Perhaps as you add each bead you recite a prayer or intention for the wearer.

- Check the length by wrapping it around your wrist as you go, leaving about an inch of cord free on each side for tying.

- Once all the beads are in place tie the ends together. Pull the knot tight and make sure it is secure.

- Option to dab a tiny bit of super glue onto the knot to keep it from untying.

- Snip off any extra cord close to the knot.

Mourning movement

Begin in a comfortable seat on the floor or in a chair. Let your spine grow tall, while you anchor down through your seat.

Allow your eyes to grow heavy or close. Let the muscles of your face relax with ease.

Bring awareness to your breath. Begin taking slow deep breaths in through the nose and out through the mouth.

Rest one hand over your heart. Inhale to feel the rising, exhale to feel the falling. If it feels right, welcome this prayer *I receive love.*

Bring in a soft flow. Take a big breath in, then on your exhale slowly bow your chin toward your chest. With your next inhale, lift your gaze toward the sky. Continue with your own gentle pace, lowering the chin with the exhale and lifting again with the inhale.

Gently return your head to center. Take a deep breath in, as you exhale, let your right ear fall toward your right shoulder. Breathe here for a few cycles. Inhale back through center, then exhale, letting your left ear fall toward your left shoulder. Rest here for a few breaths.

Bring your head back to neutral. Inhale fully. On the exhale, draw your shoulders down and back, easing them away from the ears. Inhale, lift the shoulders up towards the ears. Exhale, roll them down again. Continue this circular flow, noticing where you may be carrying tightness across the tops of your shoulders.

Return to center. Let your fingertips reach out beside your hips. With an inhale, sweep your arms overhead like a rainbow, pressing palms together at the top. Exhale, bring the hands down through your centerline, thumbs resting against your heart. Inhale again, arms sweeping overhead. Exhale, palms return to prayer at the heart. Continue moving with the breath. *I receive love.*

Welcome any other movements your body might be seeking in this moment.

When you feel complete, return to your breath. Sit comfortably for a few moments. Acknowledge any feelings or emotions that arose. Bring your hands together in a prayer resting at your heart. Gently bow your mind down to your heart in gratitude for this mourning movement.

sigil

PRAYERS

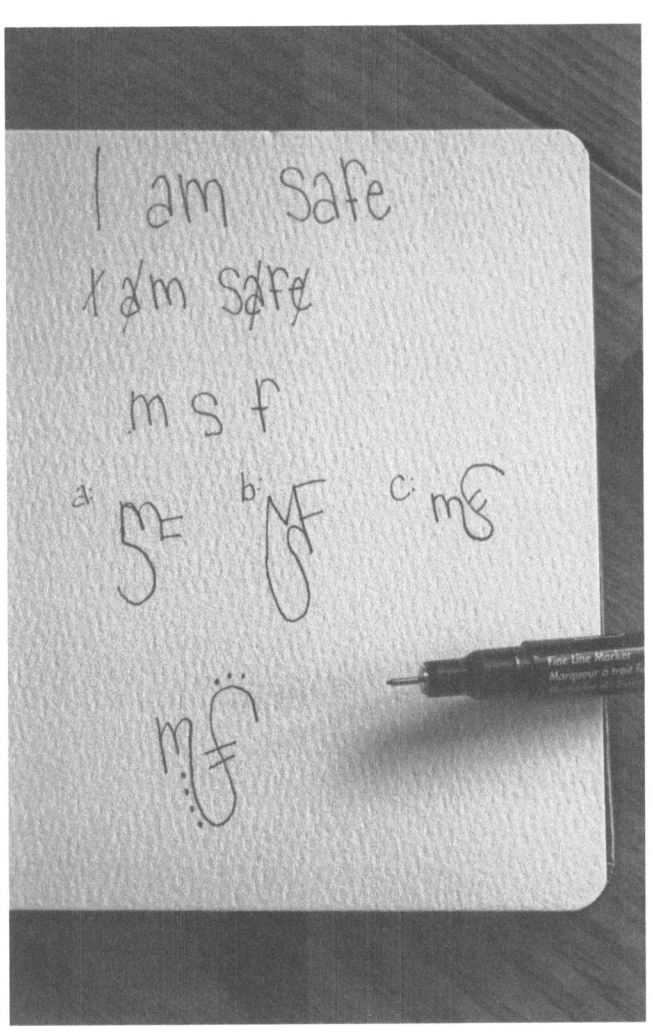

SIGIL

A Sigil is a magical symbol that represents an intention. It refers to a symbolic representation of what we yearn to manifest or alter in one's life. The seal we create invokes a new sense of renewal, thought, and imagery. It will be created condensing the letters of our intention into a monogram and then charging the sigil implanting the intention into the unconscious mind.

In grief it is helpful to create a phrase that we wish to invoke. An affirmation is a clear statement that can help you disperse dis-ease or uneasy feelings in the mind or body.

What makes this piece sacred is that it comes from you. It is created from your heart and your deepest desire. Tapping into the energy of the heart center when it is already broken open can reveal an energy that is truly holy.

YOU'LL NEED

A piece of paper and something to write with.

- Start by reflecting on the feeling you'd like to call in. What energy are you seeking? You might begin with the words I am... and allow the rest to unfold.

- Write down your intention on the piece of paper. For example: I am safe.

- From your phrase cross out any vowels and duplicate letters so you're left with a unique set.
  Example: I A M S A F E > ~~I~~ ~~A~~ M S ~~A~~ F ~~E~~ > M S F

- Below, write the letters you have leftover clearly.
  Example: M , S , F

- Rearrange, overlap, and stylize the shapes of the letters until they form a unique design.

- Simplify your sketch until it feels balanced, powerful, and visually striking. Trust your intuition.

Charging your sigil

Take a comfortable seat in front of your sigil.

Bring your palms together and begin rubbing them together generating a sensation of heat.

With warm hands hover your palms over and above your sigil.

Visualize drawing breath into your sigil. Linger here for a few moments.

Now, slowly trace a finger over the sigil. Speak out loud your intention or prayer.

As you trace your finger upon the sigil visualize a white light leaving the tip of your finger and filling the lines of the sigil. Flow through this movement with gentle repetition.

When the moment feels right, move your sigil with care to a window, letting it rest in the light of the sun or moon to charge.

Close your eyes. Envision and seal your sigil in your mind. Imagine yourself or your loved one obtaining what you yearn to manifest.

Imagine the spell has been given and received.

prayer flags

PRAYERS

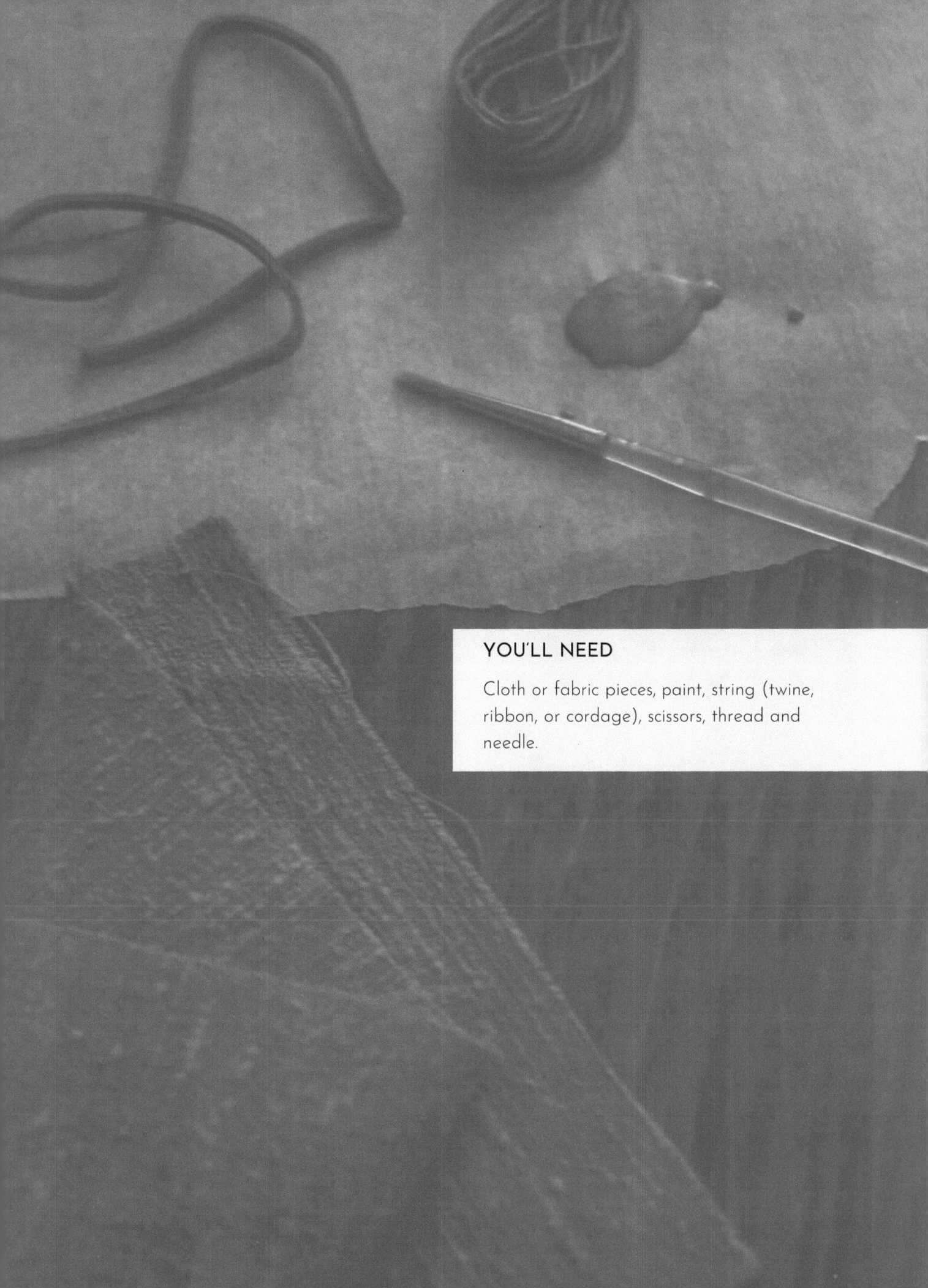

YOU'LL NEED

Cloth or fabric pieces, paint, string (twine, ribbon, or cordage), scissors, thread and needle.

PRAYER FLAGS

Prayer flags are cloth pieces painted with prayers and symbols, then hung so their blessings and energy flow outward moving gently through the surrounding space. Consider the atmosphere you want to cultivate in your space. What words, prayers, or affirmations speak to your heart and those you share it with?

- Cut your cloth into desired shape. Size is up to you. Leave 2-3 inches at the top as you will fold that down and sew at the end.

- Place the fabric over parchment paper to catch any paint that seeps through.

- Take a moment to reflect on the energy you want the flags to carry. Think about prayers, blessings, or positive wishes for yourself, your loved one, or your home.

- Decorate the flags using paint. You can also add drawings, patterns, or other embellishments that feel meaningful.

- Let them dry completely.

- Turn flag over. Fold over the top edge of each flag and sew.

- Loop the string you'll hang the flags on through a safety pin, then use the pin to thread the string through each flag's loop.

- Remove safety pin. Create loop at ends of string and hang in desired location.

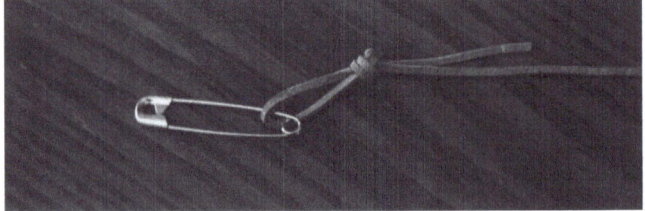

Breathless blessings

May the breath you draw in be a blessing.
Let each inhale fill you with sacred peace,
carrying the nature of divine love,
opening you to spirit's tender nearness.

With every outward breath
allow fear to fall away.
Rest in the knowing that you are capable of letting go,
and that guidance surrounds you.

In the hush where breath wanes,
a stillness holds you.
Surrender there,
in this sacred pause the body rests beyond the need for breath.

Should a yawn arrive,
receive it as a gracious release.
Allow your essence to expand,
as you drift into what cannot be seen.

With each final breath,
sip softly from this world
and exhale into the next.
The soul unbinding,
rising from body into the realm beyond.

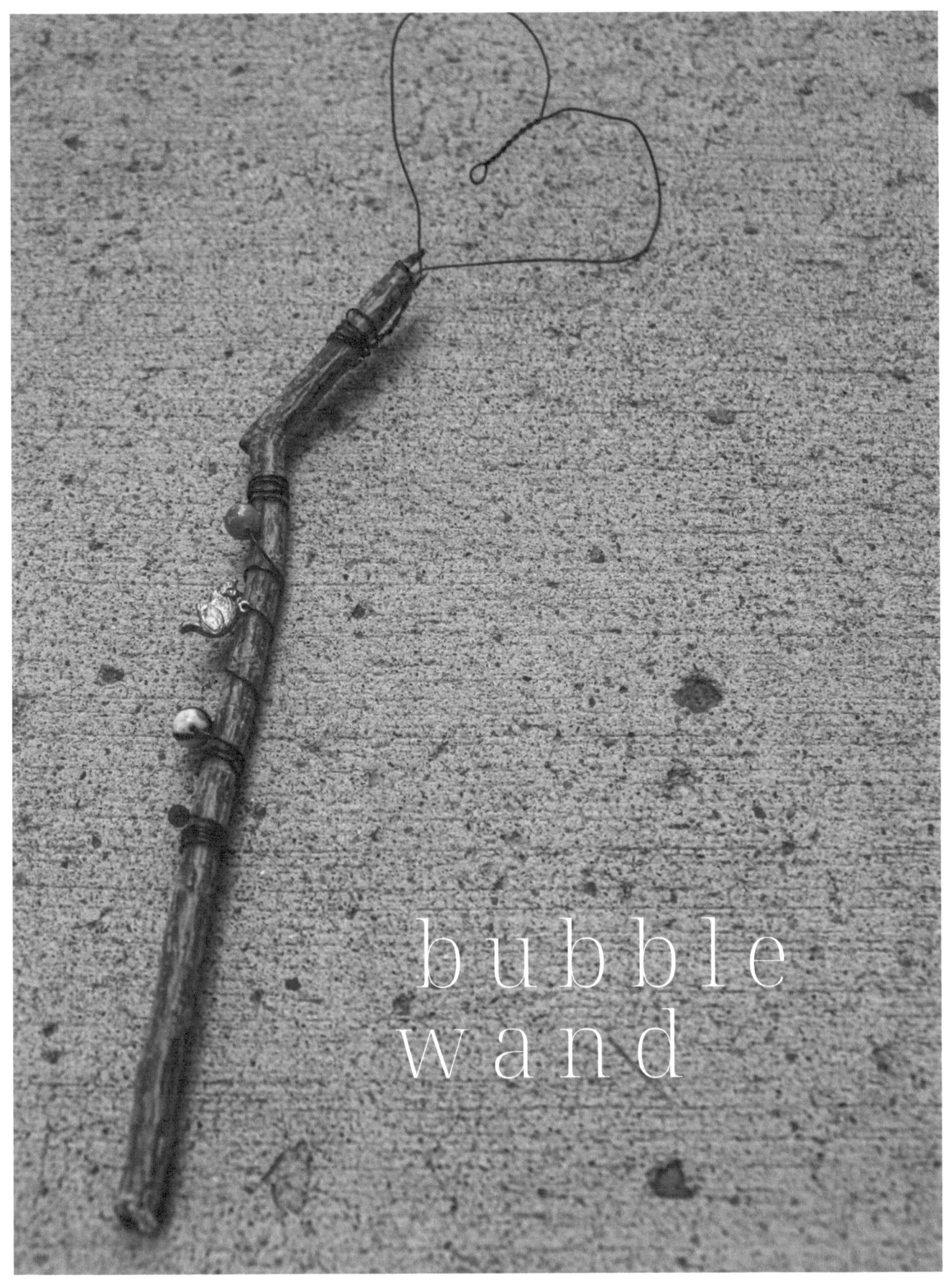

bubble wand

PRAYERS

YOU'LL NEED

A stick, beads, charms, scissors or wire cutters, floral wire, dish soap, a dish, and water.

BUBBLE WAND

Spiritually bubbles represent the release of a spirit. They symbolize the departure of the soul floating away from the physical world. Beautifully fragile they show us pure lightness in letting go and rising above.

Use your bubble wand to release prayers out, ascending into the ether. A prayer can be a wish, expressing gratitude, or sending positive thoughts.

Bubbles

- Mix water and dish soap in a short bowl. The dish should be wide enough for the wire heart to be fully submerged.

Wand

- Trim a piece of wire to be the desired length to wrap around the stick.

- Thread beads and charms onto the wire, then coil it around the stick and secure.

- Cut a new piece of wire, form it into a heart shape, and secure it to the top of the stick.

- To use: dip the wire heart into the bubble solution. Lift toward your mouth and gently blow bubble. Take your time, slow and steady works best. As the bubble forms, imagine it carrying your thoughts or messages to your loved one, wherever they may be.

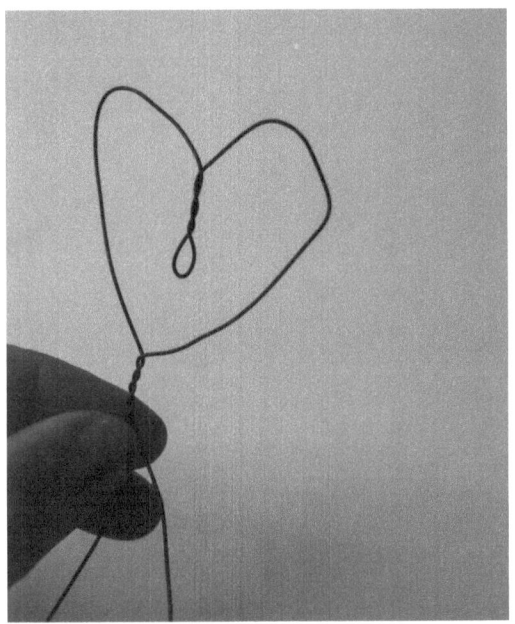

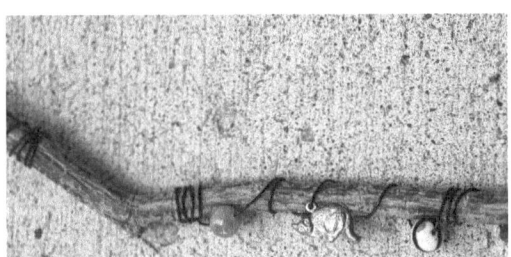

Communicating with the other side

Many bereaved feel an eternal presence of the dead and believe that we are able to continue communication with someone after death. Our relationship with them does not end, it evolves. Our connections with them move forward and transform into something unknown to us but connection is often present. Here are meaningful ways you might feel guided to connect with loved ones that have died.

Tarot

We can use tarot as a tool to potentially receive guidance and connection with our loved ones spirit through symbolic interpretation and imagery of the cards. The cards are believed to offer insight into the deceased persons energy, feelings, or messages they wish to send.

- Holding your deck in your hands, set the intention of connecting with your loved one.

- Welcome your loved one's spirit into the space and seek their guidance through the cards.

- Rest into a few deep breaths, letting yourself settle into connection with your deck. Shuffle in a rhythm that feels true, letting each movement carry your intention and presence of your loved one.

- Trust your intuition. When the moment feels right select three cards and place them upright in a row before you.

Card one representing the person passed.
Card two a lesson they would like to share.
Card three a message they would like to give.

Journaling

Writing to our loved one in a journal can be a healing practice, allowing us to speak to them as if they were still here beside us. It creates a space to share words, memories, and questions for them, even though they are no longer physically here. It aids as a way to process your grief and creates a sense of an evolving connection with them.

Signs

Signs are all around if you are open and receptive to subtle occurrences in our environment. When we ask for a sign from our loved one it is best to be specific. For example, while my cat Eleanor was dying one of the signs I asked her to send me were anything the color of her eyes. After she died she started sending vibrant green light reflections in the shape of an eye from sun catchers around our home. When I see her eyes I know that she sends me the reminder that she is still here with me in spirit.

Pendulum

When using a pendulum to speak with spirits we use specific yes or no questions and determine their messages with the pendulums movement (like swinging back and forth, circular motion, or stillness).

- Begin settled in, grounded, and with intention.

- Holding your pendulum determine which movement will be no (e.g., swing the pendulum forward and back) then yes (swing the pendulum side to side).

- Guide the pendulum back to center and stillness, then clearly ask your loved one what is on your heart.

- Remain steady and still. The pendulum may start to naturally move.

- Should you feel your question has been answered, offer gratitude and gently return the pendulum to stillness.

Meditation

When we are deep in meditation we may experience a connection with our loved one while bringing attention to a specific memory, resting in their presence, or envisioning them surrounded by peace and tranquility. Allow whatever feelings to arise.

- Bring your attention to your heart.

- Imagine that you can connect to your loved ones through your heart center.

- Create an openness to receive this connection.

- Tune in and sense their nearness.

travel altar

PRAYERS

YOU'LL NEED

Small holding container, acrylic paint or stain, Mod Podge, paint brushes, mini vessels, tea light, matches, tiny treasures, and anything else that calls to you.

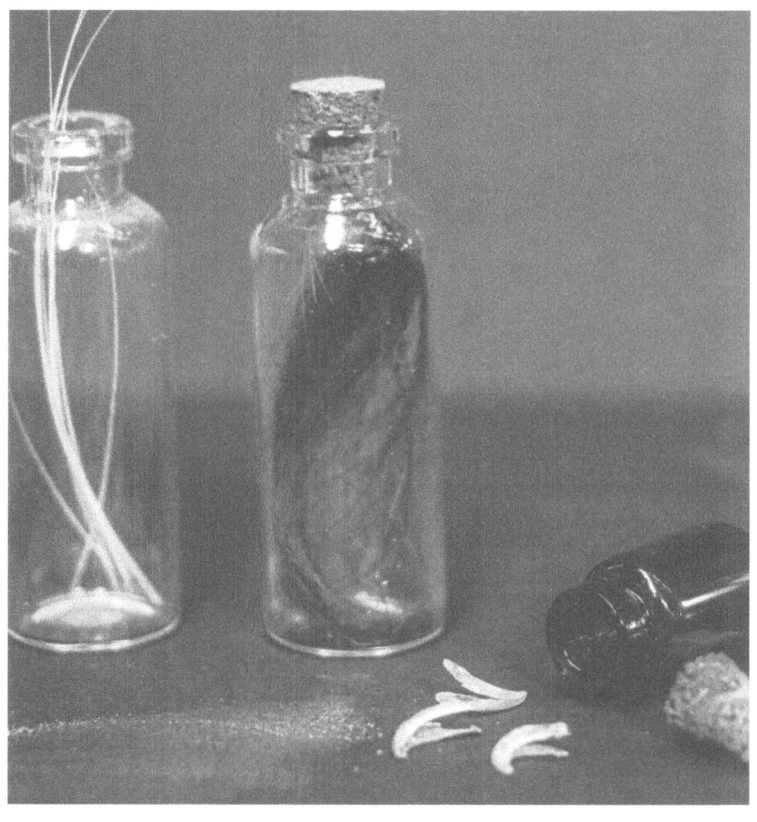

TRAVEL ALTAR

A travel altar is a tiny vessel you can carry with you, ready to be opened whenever your heart feels called. Grief often invites you into nature, whether to the river's edge, beneath the trees, or in any place you feel called. In those moments, this small altar becomes a sacred friend. Use it as a touchstone for meditation, prayer, or remembering your loved one in a new landscape.

- Choose your container. Pick something sturdy and sized for your bag or pocket.

- Make your container uniquely yours by painting, staining, or sealing with Mod Podge.

- Place tiny treasures you hold dear safe inside its walls. These small reminders are here to bring a sense of your loved one along with you on your journeys.

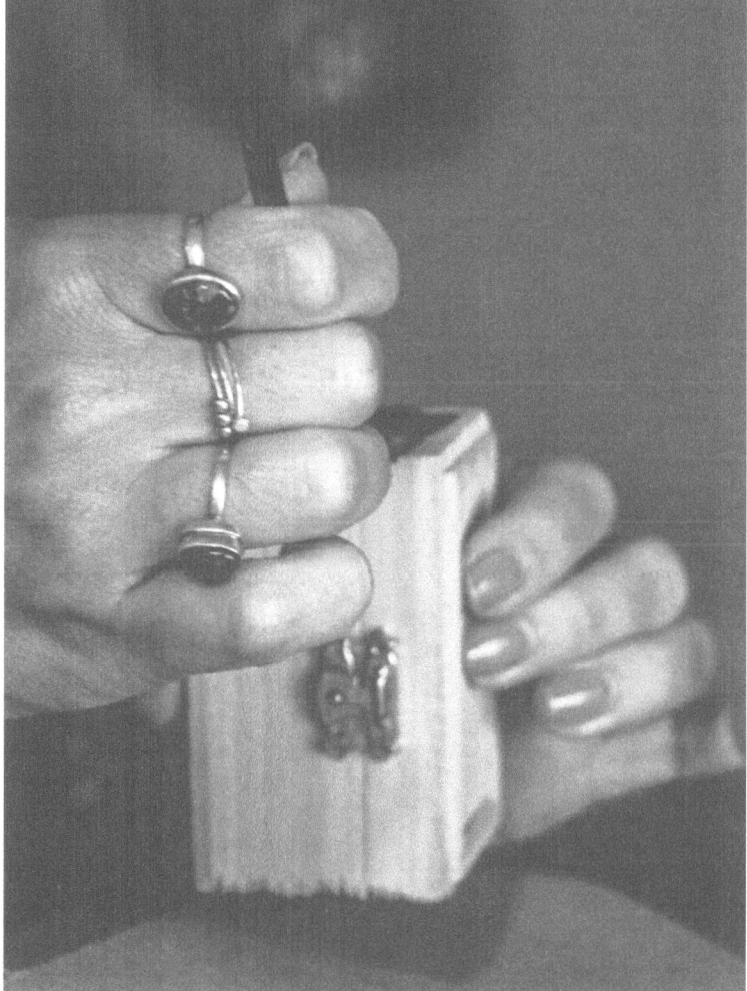

Grief-cation

No matter how far we desire to escape our grief, it will travel with us. It's common to crave distance or pause from daily life in times of sorrow. Grief often requires more time than we expect. Giving yourself extra space for respite can be healing. A grief-cation can provide a healthy outlet for mourning on your own terms. It's ok to grieve in different surroundings. You are allowed to return to daily life gradually, when you are ready.

Trip tips

- Intentionally choose your change in scenery. Seek a soft space to land.

- Grieving can feel crowded and overstimulating. You may wish to embrace the silence of solo travel. Time alone gives you the chance to find yourself again.

- On the contrary, it may feel nice to have a grief travel buddy. Someone you can share your journey with physically, support, and grieve together.

- Self nurture. You deserve it. Receiving bodywork, resting, and consuming warming meals are great ways to support your self care practice.

- Breathe and reset.

- Immerse yourself in nature. Moving our bodies out in nature aids in reducing anxiety, depression, and improves concentration. Cognitive fog during grief is common and real.

- Include activities meant to honor the life lost. Take part in an activity they liked to do. Connect with their past, loved ones, and places they held dear.

- Moments of beauty and glimmers of joy can coexist in your grief. It's ok to notice and appreciate what brings you peace.

- Welcome the tender, unpredictable waves of sorrow as it arises on your journey. Let your heart carry what it carries.

vigil votive

PRAYERS

VIGIL VOTIVE

A vigil votive is used to keep watch over a loved one in their final moments. This candle represents a heartfelt promise to stay spiritually present with someone who is dying. Its light symbolizes the enduring flow of prayer, love, and intentions. The gentle dance of the votive's flame can draw us inward, guiding us toward stillness and a meditative presence.

- Prepare your candle making supplies. Lay down parchment paper to protect the surface beneath.

- Fill pot half way with water and turn on stove.

- Measure and put your wax into a metal pouring container.

- Once the water is boiling, place the pouring container directly inside of the large pot and melt wax.

- Fragrances can be added after the wax has fully melted, preferably light, clean, and soothing scents.

- Place and stabilize the wick in the middle of the candle holder.

- Pour the wax carefully into the candle holder, leaving some room at the top to prevent overflow.

- Allow the wax to cure. This may take several hours.

- Trim wick and light.

Candle Making Safety *
Use caution with hot wax. Never leave melting wax or lit candle unattended. Keep children at a safe distance. Use tools and equipment carefully. In case of burns, run affected area under cool water and seek medical attention if needed.

YOU'LL NEED

Heat-safe candle holder, wax, stove, metal pouring container, pot, water, wick, wick holder, parchment paper, and fragrance oils if desired.

Keeping vigil

Keeping vigil is an ongoing ritual not bound to time, a devotion we can return to regularly. It is the act of sitting in the presence of our loved one when our heart feels heavy.

Set up a sacred space choosing a devotional area that feels good. This space can be indoors or outdoors.

Decorate an altar using candles, photos, letters, flowers, and special treasures.

Establish a rhythm of returning. Perhaps each evening at the hour of their passing.

Allow yourself to sit in silence, prayer, or reflection.

Draw your awareness to the treasures on your altar. Take in each item with focus and begin to reflect. Remember your loved one.

In keeping vigil, we open ourselves to what may arise: a sign from our loved one, a memory resurfacing, the presence of our beloved, or emotions seeking release.

<u>Tender gestures you can do while keeping vigil</u>

- Light a candle.

- Write letters, journal entries, or messages to your loved one.

- Hold or touch a keepsake, like a piece of clothing, jewelry, or a memento.

- Revisit photos of your loved one, noticing small details.

- Speak to them as though they were sitting beside you.

- Inhale the fragrance of their clothing, blanket, or favorite scent.

- Draw, paint, or craft in their honor.

lovey

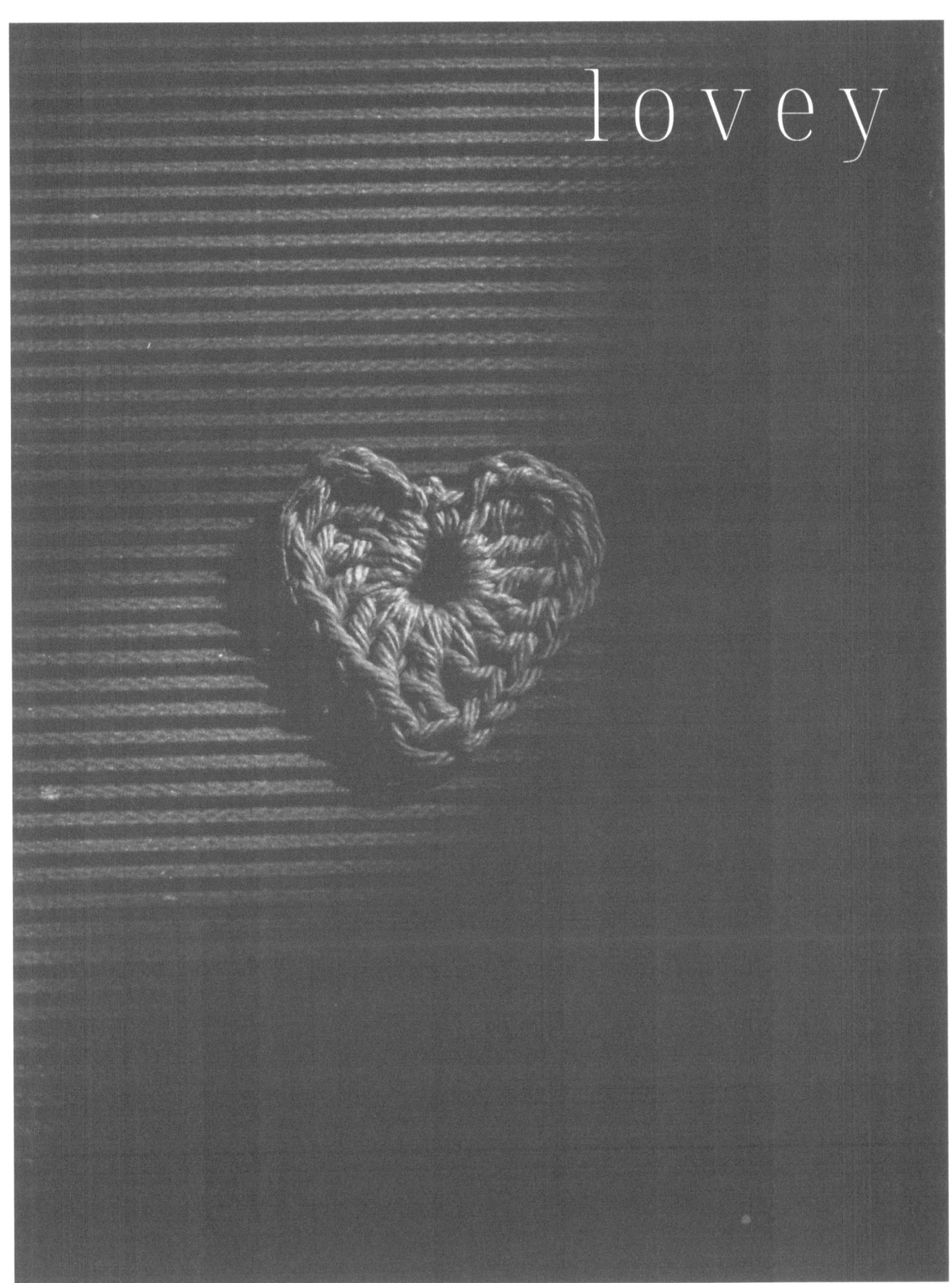

PRAYERS

YOU'LL NEED

Crochet hook, yarn, crochet needle (for weaving in ends), and scissors.

LOVEY

The art of crochet can serve as a restorative meditative practice. Crafting with both hands calms the mind, takes away distractions, and relieves stress. As you get into a rhythm and become comfortable with the repetitive motions you are invited to sit with your feelings here. Listen to your mind and what emotions arise. There is an offering in this practice to settle into mindfulness allowing us to process feelings.

A lovey is an object that one becomes attached to when seeking comfort. They help us feel safe providing solace in time of transitions to new and unfamiliar experiences. Gift your heart to yourself, the dying, or the bereaved. It serves as a token and reminder of eternal love.

<u>Warning: Choking hazard. Supervision is required if your loved one explores putting random objects in their mouth due to confusion about what items are meant for.</u>

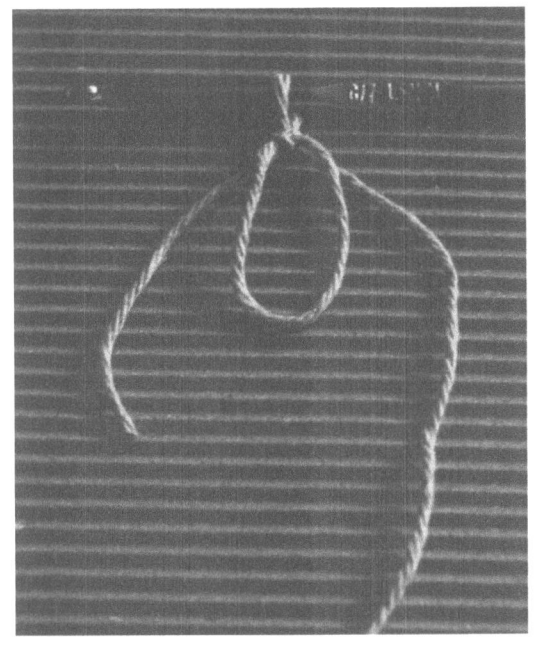
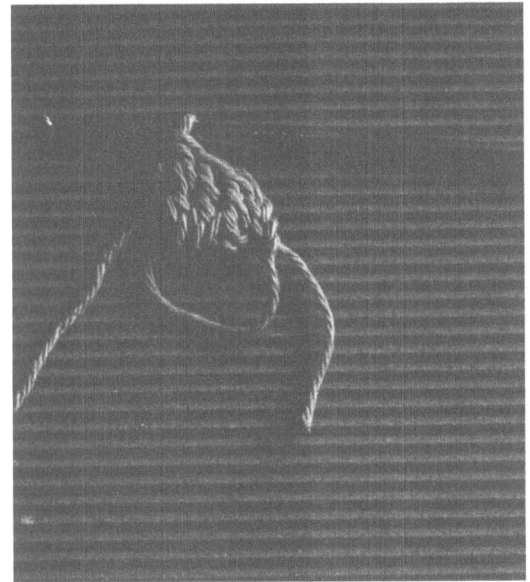

- Foundation: create a magic ring.

- Chain 2, place 3 Treble crochet inside the magic ring.

- 3 Double Crochet inside of the magic ring. Chain 1.

- 1 Treble Crochet in the magic ring. Chain 1. Half of heart is now complete.

- 3 Double crochet inside the magic ring.

- 3 Treble crochet in the magic ring. Chain 2.

- Slip stitch into the magic ring. Chain 1.

- Cut yarn while leaving a long tail. Pull tail tight.

- Close magic ring and weave in ends.

Comfort care for the end of life

At the end of life, comfort care seeks to bring ease and dignity. Simple gestures of care often carry profound weight, touching both grief and healing. Here are some helpful ways to honor and recognize this tender care.

Comfort and dignity

- Create a comfortable environment (see Death Nest page 143).
- Help them into comfortable positions when they are unable to do so themselves.
- Maintain routine activities such as eating, drinking, bathing, and toileting.
- Provide pain management. Pay attention to their subtle non verbal signals such as facial expressions, body language, vocalizations, and breathing (rapid, short).
- Ease discomfort with touch, massage, scent, and soothing sound.
- Respect their need for privacy.

Provide emotional support

- Keep them company. Read to them. Talk to them. Simply share space.
- Talk through what is happening. It can be a confusing time for them.
- Give physical contact. Hold their hand. Have a cuddle. Kiss their cheek.
- Support the physical changes they are experiencing.
- Reassure them that you will advocate and honor their wishes.
- Ensure their needs are met.

Offer closure

- Say goodbye.
- Resolve any differences.
- Talk about how their legacy will live on.
- Forgive grudges.
- Express your love and appreciation.

LEGACY

LEGACY

> Every death has a story; by telling it over and over, it will align the ineffable experience you felt in your bones and your being and help form it into words to make it feel real and more natural. There is a play between body, mind and being (or spirit) when processing feelings of loss. The stories of death need to be spoke into the earthly plane, from mouth to ear to heart.
>
> Anne-Marie Keppell
> Death Nesting

A legacy is the impression a person leaves reaching beyond their physical existence. It is a heartfelt way of keeping their story alive by weaving memory into a form of remembrance. A legacy project is a creative way to preserve wisdom, essence, and the values that shaped our lives. Whether for yourself or for someone dear, a legacy serves as a way to celebrate a life while inviting a sense of comfort and connection along the way.

<u>Legacy contemplations</u>

What imprint do you want to leave in the hearts of those you love?

How do you want your story to be told when you are no longer here?

What stories from your life do you hope others will continue to tell?

Is there anything you wish to say now that you haven't said before?

What traditions feel important for others to keep alive in your memory?

impression medallion

LEGACY

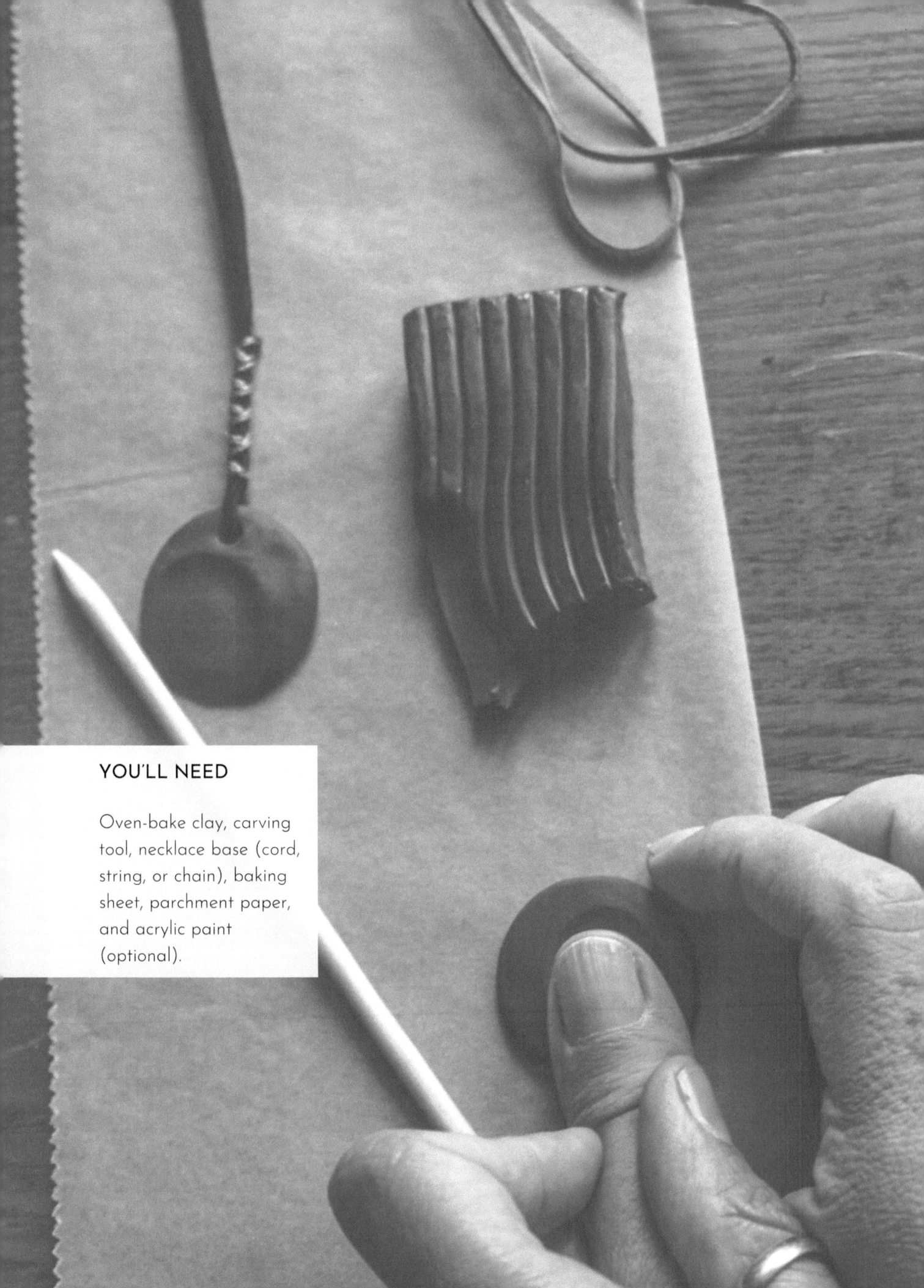

YOU'LL NEED

Oven-bake clay, carving tool, necklace base (cord, string, or chain), baking sheet, parchment paper, and acrylic paint (optional).

IMPRESSION MEDALLION

Fingerprints symbolize the imprint of presence in this lifetime. The arrangement of ridges are uniquely individual and mirror our capacity to touch others. They are reminders of the subtle ways we leave impressions on each other's lives.

As we press the fingertip into clay, the impression left leaves a signature of existence. The medallion becomes a reminder of the life lived. Their touch preserved in a talisman to adorn as you grieve the gone.

- Knead the clay until it's soft and pliable. Roll into ball, then flatten into any shape you like.

- Gently press fingertip into the clay to leave a clear imprint. Press firmly but avoid pressing all the way through.

- Carve out a hole in the top of the pendant.

- Smooth the edges.

- Place medallion on parchment-lined baking sheet. Bake according to the clay package instructions.

- Allow to cool before handling.

- Option to paint the medallion. Acrylic paints can highlight the fingerprint ridges.

- Thread cord or chain through the hole to wear as a necklace, keychain, or keepsake.

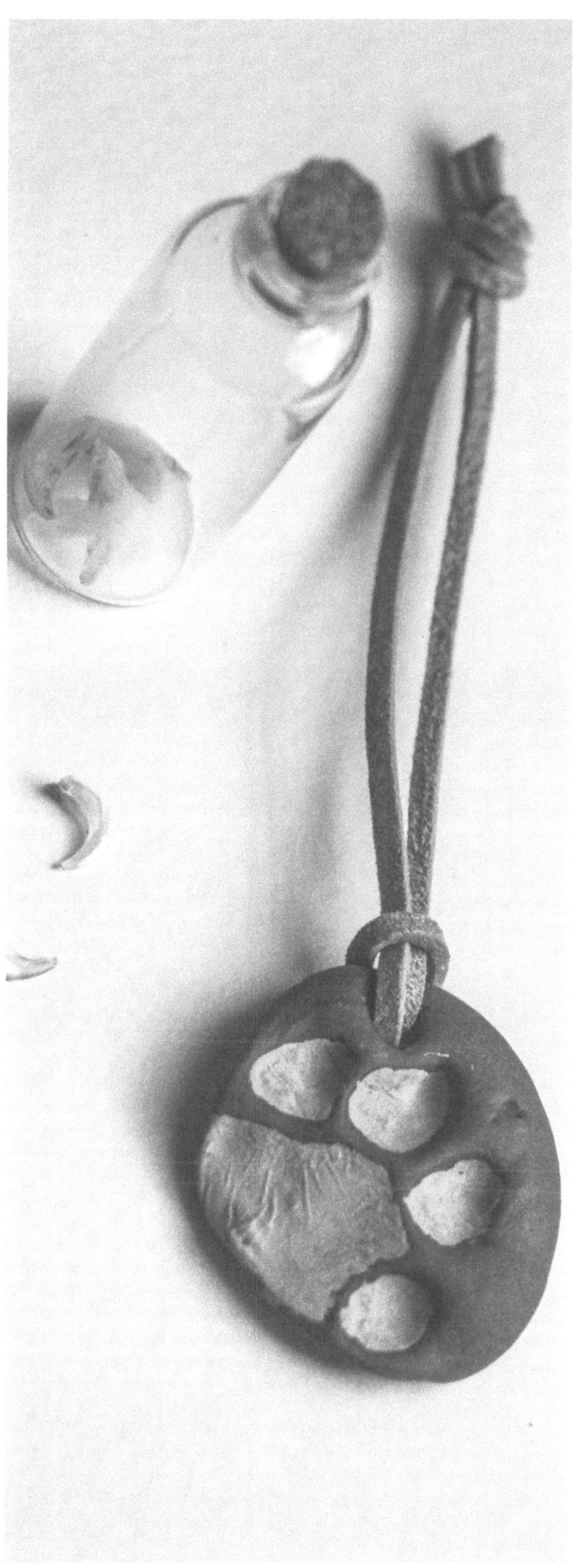

Hand remembrance meditation

Start in a comfortable resting position and begin deepening your breath.

As you anchor into this moment, set the intention of remembering your loved ones hands.

Invite your loved one in, to sit or stand before you.

Allow your gaze to rest on your their hands as they begin reaching towards you.

See the details of their hands. The slenderness or strength of their fingers. How do their nails look? Are they trimmed or long? Painted or natural?

Are there any markings that decorate their hands? Perhaps scars, birthmarks, freckles, or tattoos? Notice whether their fingers adorn rings or bands.

Now, begin to visualize your loved ones hands reaching out for your hands. Recall what it feels like as their hands hold yours. Do their hands feel warm or give of a gentle chill? Is there a softness or roughness of their palms?

Take yourself to a time or place where their hands brought you a sense of joy or comfort. Can you remember a time when their hands touched your face? Wiped away a tear?

When you are ready, slowly bring your right palm to your heart and your left palm onto your belly.

Imagine that your loved one is now behind you with their arms wrapped around you. Here, feel as if it is their hand on your heart and their hand on your belly.

In their embrace, feel into this moment....

love letter

LEGACY

LOVE LETTER

Composing a letter to someone nearing end of life is the gesture of expression when words in person may be fleeting. It is a statement from the heart offering love, closure, and connection. Letters allow us to linger in our feelings as we search for the right words and how to truly express them. There is an invitation here to pause, reflect, and communicate with clarity from the heart.

For the receiver, the letter becomes an anchor. It is something tangible they can hold, read or be read to, and find solace when time for conversing has passed. Loving words remind them of how they shaped your life and the lives of others. It reveals a sense of being remembered. Your words can help them feel safe to express their own feelings, whether joy, grief, or gratitude.

For the writer, writing a letter is an offering of saying what may be hard to speak aloud. It gives allowance for greater truth telling and vulnerability without the tender heaviness of time restriction. There's an invitation for pauses between breaths as you process your own feelings of love, grief, regret, or hope. Even if you can't be physically near the dying, your words will bridge the distance.

Writing inspirations

- Reveal a favorite memory.

- Celebrate your bond with them.

- Something they shared that will never be forgotten.

- Is there something in your heart you've yet to share with them?

- Express how they make you feel.

- Share how you'll honor their life and memory after they're gone.

- Offer words of love.

An unsent letter

How do you write a letter to someone you aren't close to? What if the dying feels more distant than familiar? What if they had already passed?

There may be unspoken words that you've held inside. Here is an invitation to write a letter without the intention of sending.

Write freely from your heart, let it all out, and surrender to the pages. Express without rules or judgment. Give voice to your thoughts, then release them through destruction. Shred the letter or tear it apart.

Writing a letter for your eyes only can be a way to process your emotions while gaining clarity without the pressure of sending it.

<u>Writing prompts for an unsent letter</u>

- A memory of you that has stayed with me is…

- You showed me how….

- A lesson I've learned in our relationship is…

- I wish we could adjust our relationship to be more like…

- Something that remains unforgivable to me is…

- I wish I would have told you…

- I will remember you as…

- Describe any emotions you have towards them.

- Reflect on anything you wish to release from this relationship.

blanket coat

LEGACY

YOU'LL NEED

A blanket, sewing machine, sewing needle, thread, fabric scissors, sewing pins, measuring tape, and binding (optional).

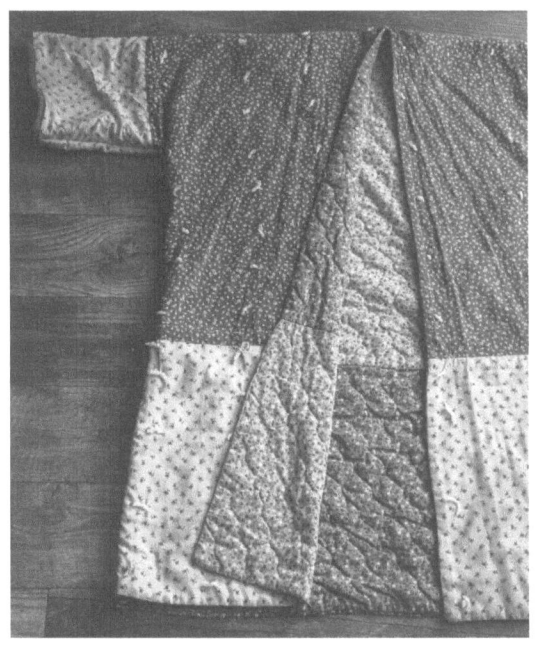

BLANKET COAT

Up-cycling blankets not only benefits the planet, but also offers a heartfelt way to breathe new life into these already beautiful pieces.

Repurposing a blanket heirloom into a wearable coat blends sustainability, sentiment, and artistry into a meaningful act. Instead of being hidden away, the heirloom becomes part of your daily life, wrapping you in warmth and remembrance. You'll carry stories from past generations, allowing you to adorn your family's history close to your heart.

This simple box coat is easy to create and the measurements can be easily adjusted for your specific desired dimensions.

- Mend any holes or damaged sections.
- Measure and cut desired pieces.
- Align and pin pieces together.
- Sew top shoulder sections.
- Sew bottom of sleeve to bottom of waist.
- Add binding if needed to any loose ends that are needing a cleaner finish.
- Wear and love your new coat.

TOP SHOULDER SECTION

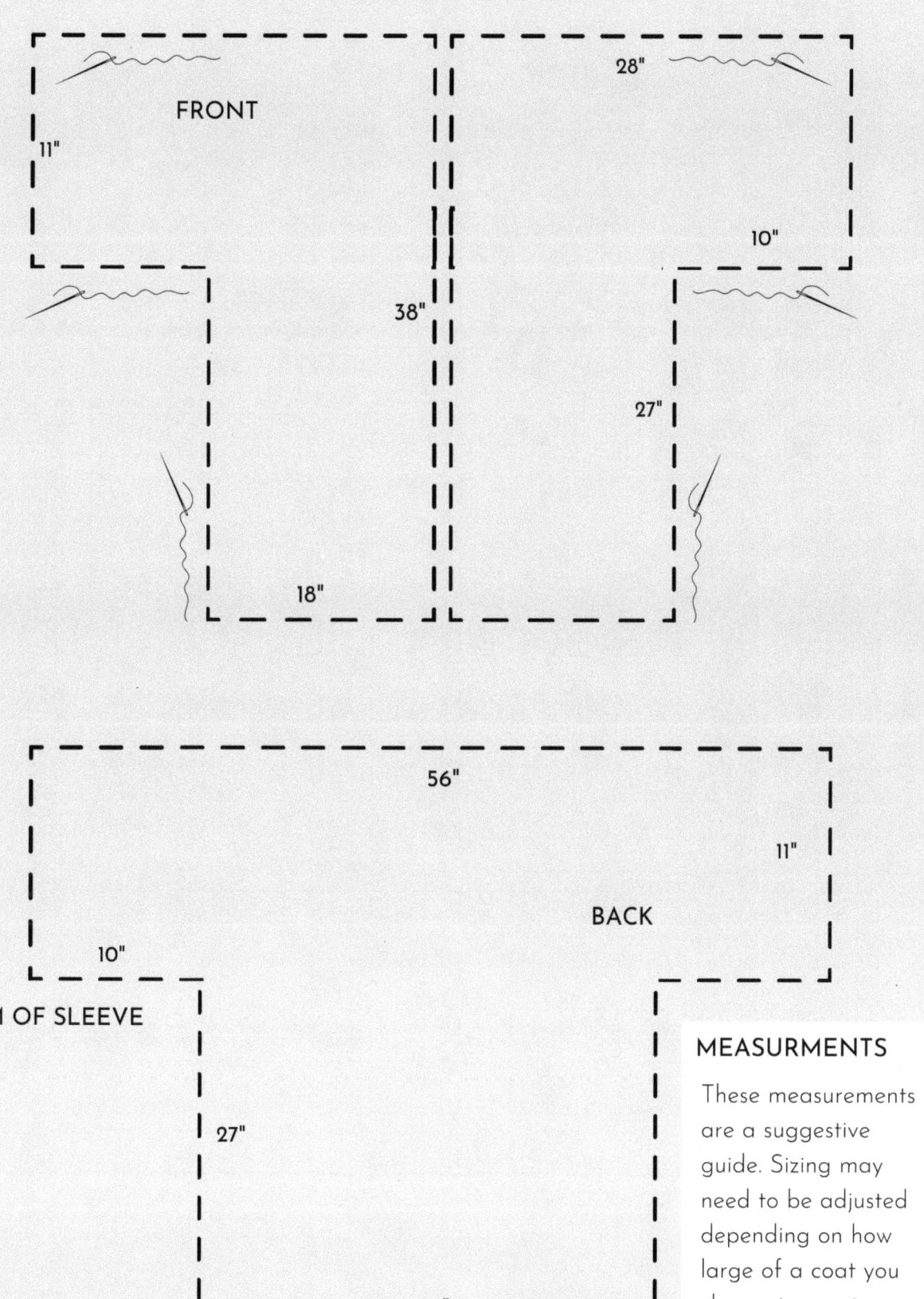

MEASURMENTS

These measurements are a suggestive guide. Sizing may need to be adjusted depending on how large of a coat you choose to create.

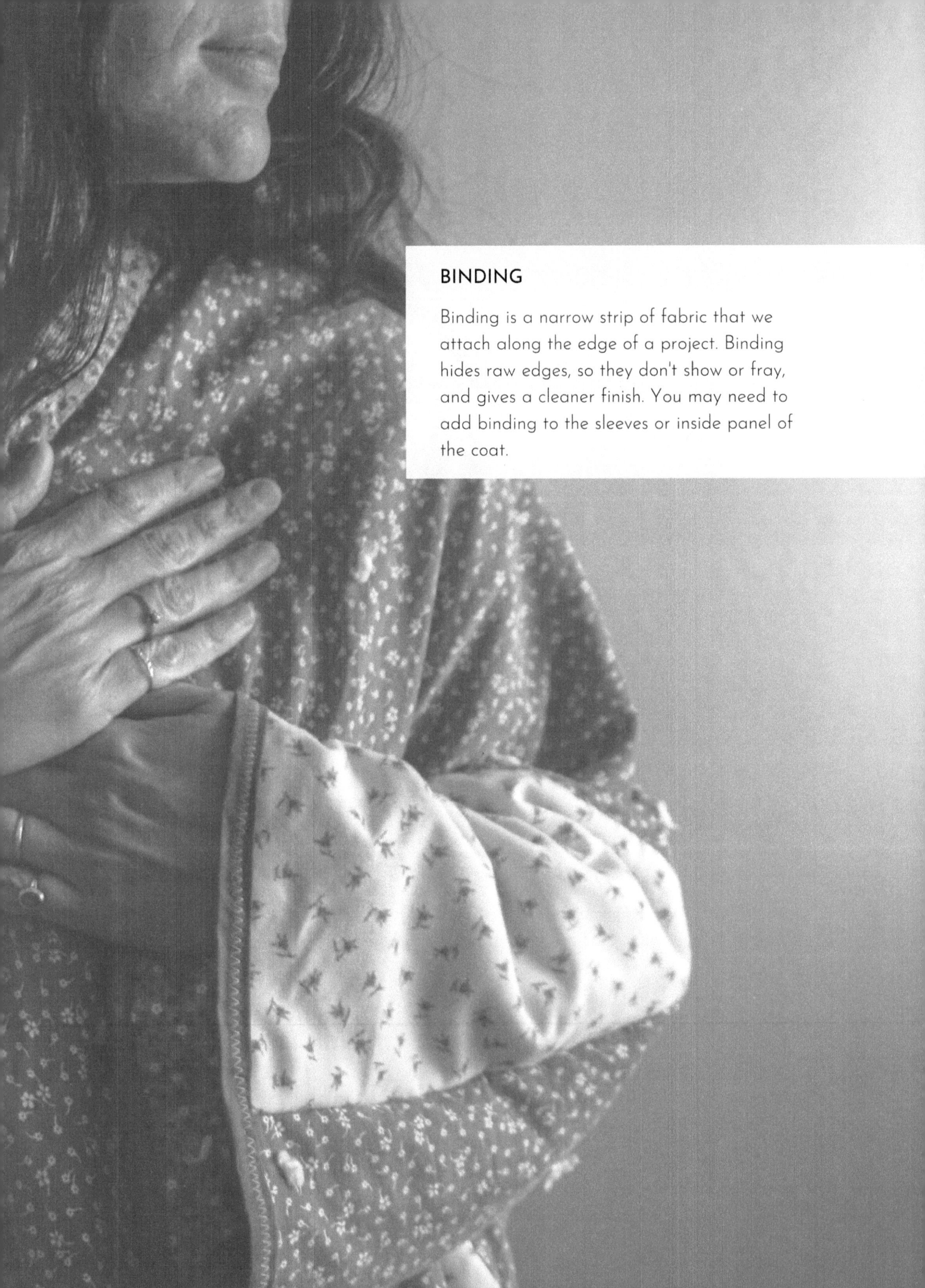

BINDING

Binding is a narrow strip of fabric that we attach along the edge of a project. Binding hides raw edges, so they don't show or fray, and gives a cleaner finish. You may need to add binding to the sleeves or inside panel of the coat.

Mourning wear meditation

Sit or lay in comfortable position.

Cocoon yourself in your mourning wear. Perhaps you drape yourself in a blanket or piece of clothing they loved.

Close your eyes and begin taking deep breathes in through the nose and out through the mouth.

Notice the sensations of the fabric as it touches your skin. Is it light or weighty? Warm or cool? Does it drape freely or hold you close?

Sense the smells that surround you. Do they awaken memories or feelings of your loved one?

Fold your arms around your body. Embrace yourself, as if your loved one was holding you close.

Call to mind the sensations you nestled in the back of your heart. Inhale softly, sending tenderness to this place. With an exhale, breathe out any tension.

Now, imagine you and your loved one are connecting heart to heart. A white light shines from the center of your chests, growing larger and more luminous with every breath.

Remember here, their presence remain with you always, residing forever in your heart.

Remain held in this experience for however long feels right....

FAMILY TREE

A family tree is a collage representation of your ancestry and the relationship between family members. Imagine, a sturdy sheet of paper or canvas becoming the soil for your family story. At its center, rests ancestors from long ago, with branches stretching outward. Pressed flowers and leaves unfurl holding a photograph of kin. These are foliage of a memory.

This is more than a family tree. It is a tapestry of faces and petals, of ancestry pressed tenderly between the pages of time. It becomes a legacy to be passed from hand to hand, so that generations yet to come may know not only the names, but the beauty, that flows through their roots.

YOU'LL NEED

A sturdy paper base (eg,. cardstock, water color paper, or even a small canvas), scissors / exacto knife, acrylic paints or watercolor (optional), copies of family photos, photo-safe glue or double-sided tape, pressed dried flowers / leaves, and tweezers.

- Choose your photos and make printed copies, never use originals. Trim them to shape.

- Select pressed flowers and leaves.

- Option to paint background and allow to dry.

- Arrange pressed flowers, leaves, and photos first without gluing. Use tweezers for delicate placement. Secure with a thin layer of glue. Be careful not to oversaturate.

- Option to write names, birth / death dates, or short captions.

- Allow everything to dry.

- Option to frame and display.

- You might consider creating additional copies of the family tree to share with loved ones, allowing its medicine to ripple outward.

Reflections from family roots

What does being in your family mean to you?

Which ancestor's life or experiences do you find yourself drawn to, and what about them speaks to you?

Describe joyful remembrance of a family gathering.

Do you see any particular talents or strengths that appear repeatedly across generations in your family?

How have the stories and experiences passed down through your family shaped who you are today?

How would you describe your family upbringing?

Describe a time when your family overcame a great challenge.

What stories have been passed down through your family line?

Describe a time when your family made you feel particularly proud.

What are some important family traditions or rituals that are still practiced today?

Are there any missing pieces in your family tree that you're curious to uncover?

photo
album

LEGACY

PHOTO ALBUM

A photo album is a vessel holding a collection of printed memories. It becomes an offering to share your loved one's story through snapshots of their journey earth side. Photos are how we are seen through each other's eyes. The portraits hold impressions that will last for a long time.

For the dying

Reminiscing on photos provides emotional comfort by bringing a sense of peace and connection as they're reminded of special moments. Seeing familiar faces may awaken memories, keeping their mind engaged and rooted in lived experiences. Conjured memories can evoke feelings of nostalgia providing a sense of comfort, reduce feelings of fear, and reinforces the presence of love. Looking back at photos together strengthens our bonds by encouraging us to share stories and emotions, resulting in a touching and memorable final shared moment.

For the bereaved

Creating an album as legacy is a beautiful way to grieve while reliving your moments together. It is an invitation of turning sorrow into a celebration of their life as you revisit cherished moments within the pages of the album. Looking at old photos helps keep their memory alive while acknowledging their absence. Photographs allow us to see our loved one's face, expressions, and gestures, helping us feel connected to them, especially when we begin to feel those memories fading.

Offerings on how to create and organize a meaningful photo album

- Choose a theme or structure. You may want to create an album chronologically (e.g., early life to end of life) or thematic (family, friends, us).

- Compile a collection of meaningful photos.

- Consider adding captions or stories.

- Invite family or friends to contribute photos or memories.

- Use pockets or envelopes in the album to hold small keepsakes.

- Option to create a digital album or slideshow for easy sharing.

Embodied memory practice

Beneath grief lives the tender fear of forgetting. A quiet dread of a slow fading of details we cherish most. The sound of their voice. The feel of their touch. The shape of their smile. The feeling of being with them. You may find yourself in times when the memories are clear as day and then others murky as mud.

Embodied memory practice is a way of calling upon the body to hold and awaken memories. The body itself becomes a vessel for remembering. The practice invites us to use movement, touch, and sensation to hold, recall, and preserve our connection to our loved ones.

Below are embodied ways of remembering

- Calling forth their motions: Letting your body repeat the subtle gestures they once made. Inviting back the little movements that made them who they were. For example, the way they held a cup of coffee. The playful lift of their eyebrow when something caught their attention. Moving your hand the way your loved one would touch your cheek.

- Walk familiar paths: Retracing the walks you once shared and areas they would visit often.

- Touching objects with movement: Hold on to something of theirs allowing your body to sway, cradle, and rock with it slowly.

- Gentle dance of memory: Revisit motions you experienced together allowing your body to move the way you used to move together.

- Restorative stillness: Lying down or resting in a way you remember being near them.

- Movement based practice: Engage the body in physical activity like yoga, dance, somatic ritual, and walking meditations. Offer this practice in their honor as a tribute to them.

- Smell, taste, and sound: Breathe in the scents, taste the flavors, and listen to the sounds that carry their presence.

JOURNAL

You are the writer of your life's story. A journal serves as a safe-keeper and preserver of your most intimate of mind wanderings. The simple practice of recording moments becomes a safe space to acknowledge feelings, process emotions, and anchors you into the present moment. Your memories are yours alone, they're a treasure to cherish, hold on to, and reminisce upon later.

The act of journaling can motivate you and ignite a sense of purpose. Making space to journal provides ritual and rhythm creating a sacred container. It becomes an intentional space for reflection, meaning making, and creates a sense of inner order amidst uncertainty.

It captures significant moments from your life that you chose to safeguard. These books are an offering to return to, whether once a year, on a quiet day, or in life's final chapters. You are invited to revisit and relive the moments they hold. It is a way to remember past seasons, experiences, and reflect on life lived.

The words you place on these pages preserves a legacy for loved ones you leave behind. It becomes a keepsake communicated by hand and carries your voice forward for generations. Your loved ones will be able to see your writings and experience your life through your eyes. They'll hear your voice within your words and feel your heart in your stories.

<u>Whether your just beginning your journaling journey or if you're a seasoned chronicler here are some offerings you may include on your pages</u>

- Daily reflections
- Quotes
- Gratitude lists
- Memories
- Life lessons
- Milestone moments
- Goals, hopes, dreams

Daily reflections: writing prompts

What do I want to remember about today?

Today I felt...

A challenge I faced and overcame today was...

A moment today that made me smile was...

Today I am grateful for...

What could I learn from today?

The most meaningful part of today was...

Describe what you did to relax and unwind...

How did I deal with stress today?

Something I grieved today was...

What inspired me today...

Reflect on something you feared...

Describe a memory that came to you today...

Write about how and if you are feeling supported...

Describe a time when you felt truly seen....

What was holding me back today?

Things I am proud of today...

Reminiscing: writing prompts

Write about your earliest memory in detail. How old were you? Who were you with? What was happening?

What is your most special family memory? Who was there?

What year was the best year of your life? What about the year made it so great?

What was the greatest challenge you've experienced? Why was it so hard? How did you evolve from that experience?

When was a time you felt incredibly grateful?

What life experiences shaped you?

Write about special memories of your pets.

If you have a significant other or partner write about how you first met? What was your favorite thing you've done together? How did being around them make you feel?

What is your favorite memory of food? Who made it? Is there a recipe you can share?

Who were your closest friends? How did you meet? What are your favorite memories with them?

Are there any decisions you regret making?

What was the bravest thing you've ever done?

Write about your first experience with birth.

Write about your first experience with death.

END OF LIFE PHOTOGRAPHY

Photography isn't just about capturing images. The deeper practice of photography is intentionally capturing the presence in each moment. It is the conscious act of looking beyond the lens with intention of bearing witness.

End of life photography is an honoring of capturing final moments together. The images tell a story of a dying journey. It is a testimony of observing and holding space for most likely the hardest thing our loved has ever done. When we photograph these raw moments we share their story, struggle, and vulnerability. We honor their path.

End of life photography can be a beautiful way to celebrates a life's transition and will be emotional. Commemorative photos give us the gift to capture memories to cherish after our loved one has died. A physical photo can hold energy and bring us comfort. Having photos of your loved ones final moments is a special keepsake you can hold on to and revisit when you're missing them.

End of life photos can also help others on a similar path. Death does not look like what is shown in movies, far from it. If we have not already witnessed the reality of death up close when we reach a point to where we have to see it, it can be unfamiliar and unknown. Facing the unforeseen in the death portal can leave us feeling uneasy and overwhelmed.

Seeing intimate photos of end of life journeys helped prepare me for what I may inevitably see on our journey. It was seeing an emaciated body, sinking eyes, and fragile skin that shed light on how the body changes towards death. Home funerals, shrouding rituals, and ceremonial washing of the body helped me visually understand and prepared me for the appearance of the body in transition and after death. Seeing images of others grieving helped me feel less alone and more connected to the human experience of death and dying.

Not every moment needs to be captured. There's a quote in the movie The Secret Life of Walter Mitty that replays in the back of my mind often.

"Sometimes I don't [take a picture]. If I like a moment, for me, personally, I don't like to have the distraction of the camera. I just want to stay in it, right there, right here." - Sean O'Connel (Sean Penn)

I come back to this quote when I reach for the camera but question when a moment feels too sacred and should only be seen through eyes and not through film. Lean into your intuition. Through end of life photography there is an invitation to be mindful of these moments, seal in the sacred, and preserve the memories in your mind.

When capturing photographs at the end of life, you might notice

- Intimate moments: You may see pure emotions such as sadness, anger, and confusion. It is recommended to be emotionally ready to process the range of emotions that may come up. Give yourself space to process the sensations.

- The physical decline of the person: You may be able to witness a trend in their body gradually becoming smaller and frail. Weighing the dying may become challenging therefore taking weekly or monthly photographs may help visually see how their body transforms. You may see sunken eyes, pronounced bone structure, emaciation, and change in skin. Close up photos allows us to capture details in their hands and face that we cherish or wish to remember.

- Changes in behavior: Capturing moments of things they did often to them doing it less often. You may see a decline of laughing, smiling, or even a playful eyebrow raise.

- Focus of attention and declining cognitive function: A common change at the end of life is the dying may have a change in focus and attention. It is a shift towards difficulty concentrating. You may notice confusion or a decreased awareness of their surroundings.

- Moments of pure radiance: You could be blessed with the presence of an adoring gaze, a delicate gesture, a hint of euphoria, or a light in their eye. Capturing a rare moment such as these can be a beautiful gift of legacy for their loved ones. Even, if the moment is not photographed, purely witnessing and sharing about the moment with their loved one can serve as a gift later.

- You may witness death: You may be in the room where the deceased's body rests, and that can be a bit stunning post mortem. After the last breath, the body begins to change appearance as the time after death unfolds. The body may appear waxy, stiff, and cold. The skin may show signs of change in color. Their eyes and mouth may be open. These are all natural appearances after a death has occurred.

Acts of observation
+ reflections

When taking end of life photos, an act of observation is a sacred pause. It is the intentional witnessing of a person, their presence, and the essence of their final moments. The act of observation is not just about seeing through the lens, but being with the unfolding.

<u>Prepare</u>

- Take a few minutes before you begin to ground into the present moment.

- Ensure your camera does not need a flash or intense lighting. Bright lights can be alarming and interfere with presence.

<u>Observe</u>

- Notice nuances in their behavior, body language, and demeanor.

- Let your surroundings guide you and connect with the energy of the room.

- Withhold judgement to attain a deeper understanding into their inner world.

- Approach the situation through their eyes.

- Observe in a way that makes them feel comfortable and safe.

- Uncover emotion and document the raw moments.

- Focus on the details, the people, the person, or objects around the room. Let go of expectations. Be flexible with outcomes.

- Ask mindful questions. Open ended questions encourage a deeper exploration of someones thoughts and experiences.

- Actively listen. Pay attention to what someone is saying. Notice their tone.

Reflections - Set aside time to reflect on your observations

- How did being in a death space make you feel?

- Was there anything that evoked a sense of thankfulness for the experience?

- Was there a gained deeper understanding of life's purpose?

- Were there any notable sights, sounds, or scents?

- Has facing mortality lead to a more accepting attitude towards the reality of death?

- In hindsight, was there anything you saw that you would have wanted done differently if it was your end of life journey?

keepsake case

LEGACY

KEEPSAKE CASE

A keepsake case is a memory container filled with special mementos belonging to your loved one. This small sanctuary safeguards the keepsakes that carry your loved one's essence.

This sacred box cradling their most treasured items can be taken out when you miss them most. Open when you need a sensory hug. Hold each piece with soft hands and a tender heart.

Store your case in a space somewhere accessible and where you can visit often, safe from neglect or dust.

Treasures you may wish to tuck inside your keepsake case

- Photos
- Letters
- Journals / Notebooks
- Books
- Clothing / Accessories
- Jewelry / Talismans
- Items they held dear
- Recipes

Reminiscence visualization

Settle in to a comfortable position with your keepsake case directly in front of you.

Begin by placing both palms on the top of the case. Take a moment to ground yourself and become present.

When it feels right, open the case slowly.

Focus on the case in its entirety. Direct your attention to all the items that fill its space.

Choose an item out of the case and hold it with both hands. Perhaps you hold the item close to your chest or up to your nose breathing in its scent.

As you take in the item, try to remember details this item represents during a time with your loved one.

What memory arises?

How was this piece meaningful to your loved one?

If it is something they wore try to visualize them wearing the item.

How does this item make you feel?

What is the story behind the piece?

If the item was written by your loved one imagine their voice narrating it to you.

Repeat and take your time with any items that call to you in the moment.

DEATH CONTEMPLATION

DEATH CONTEMPLATION

> You have to die all the way to be dead. And this is what scares us about it. Its finality. But in life, this is just the way it is. You have to die all the way before you can resurrect.
>
> Meggan Watterson
> Mary Magdalene Revealed

We will die. Death is a doorway we will all pass through. So many others have died and walked this path before us, and we will eventually follow. We are all just walking each other home.

Death contemplation is the practice of recognizing the impermanence of our lives and the ineffable. As we reflect on our own mortality it can lead to a gateway of liberation. When we embrace that this life has an end we begin to see the graveness of living with presence. We become awakened to the true matters of the heart.

Death contemplation embraces open and honest conversations around death and dying. It destigmatizes its view of being taboo or morbid. Death literacy becomes a movement that normalizes the grieving process and encourages death education.

Benefits of death contemplation

- Reduced fear of death.

- Preparedness and peace.

- Greater acceptance of change and impermanence.

- Clarity of values.

- Strengthened relationships.

The offerings to follow will invite you to meet the following reflections

- What does your relationship with death and dying look like?

- What would bring you peace in your final moments?

- What does your ideal death look like?

- What are your final wishes?

- What legacy do you wish to leave?

- How would you like to be remembered?

send-off shrine

DEATH CONTEMPLATION

SEND-OFF SHRINE

A send-off shrine for the dying is a sacred bedside altar created to honor the transition from life to death. It serves as a physical and spiritual container for saying goodbye, expressing love, and offering presence during a deeply sacred and vulnerable journey. A send-off shrine can help ease fear, empowering silence into connection, reverence, and peace.

As our loved one moves through the labor of dying their eyes may remain open, fixed on a single spot, or rest at half mast. Having a bedside altar close invites comfort and familiarity.

A send-off shrine can be assembled in the days or weeks before death as a part of comfort-focused care. It is an act of love and a way to hold space for what cannot be changed, only witnessed.

When creating the shrine think about what your loved one loved the most. If they are able to, ask them what items they would like included.

These offerings can be held within the altar's care

- Photos of loved ones, ancestors, or beloved places.

- Candles for light and guidance.

- Elements from nature. Perhaps flowers, stones, feathers, or shells to symbolize impermanence and beauty.

- Letters, journals, or objects that reflect their identity, passions, or legacy.

- Personal pieces such as jewelry, letters, a favorite book, or instrument.

- Small offerings as a gesture of love and farewell.

Later, the send-off shrine can transition into an angel altar. A space where the bereaved can sit, pray, and mourn the loss of our loved one.

Holding sacred silence

There may come a time when the words begin to fade and fall away, where the quiet carries the deepest truth. The following are invitations for staying in the silence as it becomes sacred.

- Offer quiet presence.

- Allow the silence to hold the weight of love and farewell.

- Sit or lay gently beside or bedside.

- Cradle their hands in yours with care.

- Breathe slowly together, honoring the stillness between heartbeats.

- Honor boundaries.

- Abstain from judgement.

- Be empathic.

- Be a safe space.

- Support their experience.

- Bear witness to their gentle releasing.

DEATH CONTEMPLATION

CROSSING THE VEIL

The veil is the curtain between the seen and the unseen. Crossing of the veil refers to the mysterious journey from a world known and entering into the unknown. It is the liminal space between earth and ether, between body and spirit.

A collage gives form to what dances beyond definition. It becomes an offering of personal interpretation, spiritual reflection, and a visual way of expressing the ineffable.

It unfolds a gentle way of exploring mortality, grief, and the mysteries of transition. Creating imagery around the veil can soften fear and anxiety around death and dying.

For those moving through mourning, a collage can be a way to feel connected to a loved one who has crossed the veil. It becomes a visual prayer, a sacred remembrance, or a symbolic bridge to the other side.

YOU'LL NEED

Scissors, craft knife, glue, double-sided tape, base surface (e.g., cardstock or cardboard), printed photos, clippings (from magazines, books, newspaper), and option for frame.

CROSSING THE VEIL

Prompt ideas to reflect on before collaging

- What do I imagine lies beyond the veil?

- What helps the soul cross gently?

- What symbols represent death, spirit, or transformation to me?

- Is there someone I feel close to on the other side?

Create the collage

- Begin gathering images, textures, or words. Be intuitive.

- Choose photos or clippings that feel aligned with your vision of death, rebirth, spirit, release, and continuity.

- Let your hands guide you. Cut, rip, or tear the images in a way that feels natural. Invite the breaking or cutting of images as a way to express transformation, grief, or letting go.

- Let each image find its way home to the background by securing it with glue or tape when it feels settled. Think of it as anchoring a vision between the seen and unseen.

- When your collage feels complete, consider honoring by framing it, scanning it, or photographing it to keep a lasting memory.

Into the ether:
a veil visualization

The following practice is offered as a way to honor final breaths and the tender space beyond.

Begin by laying down in a way that feels grounded and comfortable.
Allow your eyes to gently close, if they still close.
Come into stillness allowing the breath to settle.
Let all effort fall away.

While you settle into stillness, sense the sounds of the body.
Drop into the inner drumming of the heart,
the soft hush of the breath,
the quiet rhythms as the chest rises and falls.

There is a becoming of rest between breaths.
The space unfolds and widens as last breaths drift away.
And then... there is silence,
but not emptiness.
Rather, a soft unveiling.

May this way be lit by the stars.
May the unseen cradle you.
May the silence carry you.

Go forth, slip into the ether,
with the sky behind your back.

Enter gently into the unseen,
the realms beyond knowing.

Rest into the mystery,
carrying love within you.

DEATH CLEANING

As within, so without, your home reveals the energy of your soul. Your space reflects the essence of who you are while mirroring your internal world. While death cleaning is intended for those later in life, it can also be helpful for when we feel buried under the weight of what we've held onto. It is the process of tending to the energy of our homes and living as true to yourself. It becomes the journey of clearing out old weight ready to be lifted.

Death cleaning can be an emotional process of working through your stuff. Our homes can be filled with generations of excess. This is a time to reflect on what items you genuinely love, truly need, and what you no longer need or use, to make space to breathe. As we create spaciousness in our homes, we create room for spirit to flow.

In the heart of death cleaning it is not about getting rid of everything, but honoring the space and caring for the home as a sacred vessel. Not everything is ready to be released, and that is okay. This process is about sensing the items that still belong with us now. Keep what still feels connected to you and your story.

Hold these reflections in mind as you clear your space

- What items still speak to your heart and spirit?

- What holds special memory or meaning for you?

- What belongings feel like an extension of your story?

- What things offer comfort, insight, or remembrance?

It's natural to feel overwhelmed. It is normal to be attached to things. When it feels too heavy I invite you to ask for support from someone close to you, someone you feel safe with. Dealing with this on your own may feel isolating. Not only can their support make the path lighter, but it also offers the opportunity to be seen and witnessed.

Death cleaning gives us a certain perspective on life. When we die we can't take our physical belongings with us. Through this journey we begin the process of getting our physical belongings together so our loved one's aren't burdened with decluttering after you die. It gives us an opportunity to practice detachment and of letting go. This journey is not something to be rushed. When you are ready, take your time, go slow.

DEATH CLEANING

Soul-led suggestions to support sacred clearing

- Start small. One space, section, or room at a time.

- Go slow. Take your time with each piece. Hold it close and reflect on how you feel, how it makes you feel.

- Gift items that you are still fond of but are ok letting go of. Invite your loved ones to share if there are items they'd like to hold onto when you're gone. Not only does this help you out, it also opens the conversation up around death and dying.

- Donate to a local charity that holds meaning to you. Your things will find new homes. Letting go of items doesn't mean we are letting go of love. The love lives on in memory, not belongings.

Stewarding the space with presence and reverence

- Tend to the space with care and intention. Try your best to keep the room clean and tidy. Start simple by leading with making the bed each morning.

- Let what you already have be enough. You may not need to purchase new things. Try to curate and use what is already available to you.

- Return things to their space as an act of mindfulness.

- Treat the organization as something to be gently upheld. Honor the peace of the space by tending to it regularly.

Words of release

Letting go can be a journey and may take time. You must be present. The is no more lingering in the past or worrying of the future. It's a matter of surrender, releasing of attachments, and dissolving expectations.

For the dying, the journey of letting go is laborious as they transition away from the physical body and physical realm. Sometimes there is struggle to release while clinging to the vessel that they called home for their lifetime. The truth is, no matter how hard we want to hold onto something, the release will happen eventually... and when ready.

Offering permission to die can be a profound act of comfort and a gift of peace. It can help the dying person feel at ease, release fear, and relax them into the journey home. As much as it may physically hurt our broken heart, it can truly be a gift for the dying.

<u>Comforting words you may offer as your loved one prepares to let go</u>

My darling,
it's ok to let go.
You will be fine.
I will be fine.
We will all be ok.
You are not alone.
You are held here.
You are safe.
I am right by your side.
When you're ready, I am ready.
You can surrender now.
Let it be.
Let go.

Let go.

Let go.

death nest

DEATH CONTEMPLATION

DEATH NEST

Death Nesting is the instinctual yearning to get a space ready to prepare for dying. Just as we nest for a birth, death nesting becomes a sacred offering of mindfully designing an area that brings comfort, meaning, and connection as the body prepares for its final breaths. A death nest becomes an altar-like sanctuary of stillness. This can be in a persons home, care facility, or hospital. Wherever the space comes to be, it should feel comfortable, clean, and safe for transition. May the following offerings guide you as you gently shape a comforting and meaningful death nest that honors your loved one's journey.

Essentials for a Death Nest

Comfort

- Comfortable bed. An adjustable or hospital-style bed can provide greater comfort and accessibility at the end of life.
- Clean bedding. Multiple clean sheets and under-pads are recommended for incontinence.
- Pillows for gentle positioning.
- Eye Pillow (see Final Rest Eye Pillow page 151) or light cloth to rest over the eyes if appropriate.
- Clean and an uncluttered space.

Scent, sight, and sound

- Essential oils for calming (e.g., lavender, sandalwood, eucalyptus).
- Spray mist or anointing oil for the room or body.
- Natural sunlight, mood lighting, or candlelight.
- Liminal Soundscape (see page 147).
- Flowers and foliage to represent the beauty of impermanence and remembrance.

Personalized items

- Photographs of loved ones, ancestors, pets, or special places.
- Letters from friends and family.

DEATH NEST

- A beloved stuffed animal or handmade item.
- Treasured trinkets or momentos.

Spiritual support and meaning

- Oracle cards, affirmations, or handwritten blessings.
- Sacred texts, poems, or readings nearby.
- Guided meditation scripts.
- Spiritual talismans.

Calling in comforts

Begin laying down. Close your eyes and take a few deep breaths.

Now, gently imagine you are in your final days to hours of life.
Visualize the space forming around you.
Not just any place, but your final resting space. Your death nest.
A place where your body can release, and your spirit can rise...

What does this space look like?
Allow your imagination to guide you.

Now, begin calling in the comforts...

Call in the room you wish to die in. A room that feels like home. A room that feels safe and familiar.

Call in the presence of those you love, living or gone. Invite them to sit or lay down next to you.

Call in your death bed that will cradle your body. Call in the blankets that feel familiar, warm, or cool. Perhaps a quilt or linen that smells of home.

Call in the sounds that bring you peace. Is this a song? A chant? Nature calling? Do you hear the voices of your loved ones close by?

Call in the smells that as you inhale your body relaxes and your heart flutters.

Call in the objects that make you feel safe, grounded, and loved. These can be photographs, talismans, momentos, childhood stuffed animals, and letters. Are these items bedside? In your hand?

Call in the light. Is it sunlight, dim, or dark in your space? Do you notice the fluttering flame of a candle or feel the rays of sun on your skin?

Now, begin to feel yourself fully nestled within this sacred space.
There is only rest.
Only breath.
Only the quiet rhythm of release.

liminal soundscape

DEATH CONTEMPLATION

LIMINAL SOUNDSCAPE

Hearing tends to linger as other senses fade, offering a final connection to the world. Even in an unconscious state sound can create a sense of calmness, familiarity, and help us be aware of our surroundings. A liminal soundscape is a musical or ambient environment created to support someone in the sacred space between life and death, and becomes a sound offering for the journey home.

When choosing what melodies to integrate into the collection choose music that is familiar and meaningful to the dying. What songs do they frequently whistle, hum, or sing aloud? What tunes bring them joy or send tears down their cheeks? If they have the energy, invite your loved one to help shape their final soundscape.

At the end of life, a liminal soundscape might look like

- A personal playlist or collection of songs that feed the soul.

- Music that feels non-linear or timeless, offering comfort without demanding attention (like soft chanting, ambient tones, acoustic strums, or nature recordings).

- Sound that supports surrender, stillness, and connection.

- Alongside music, the offering of sound might include voice recordings or video blessings. This can hold just as much sacredness as music in this final passage.

Be mindful of additional background noise or side conversations. Eliminating outside noise gives the dying a chance to focus on and be in the moment with the music. Closing bedroom doors and windows allows the dying to concentrate deeper on what they are hearing. Keep awareness on volume. Softer soundscapes create a calmer energy in the death nest. Gentle volume allows for a relaxing surrounding that helps the dying alleviate agitation and prepare for restful sleep.

Purpose of a liminal soundscape at death

- Eases transition while creating a calming atmosphere.

- To mark the experience as sacred, gentle, and intentional rather than medicalized or silent.

- Evokes memory and meaning.

- Calms the nervous system by reducing fear or agitation with soothing frequencies.

LIMINAL SOUNDSCAPE

- To hold space reverently for the dying and their loved ones.

- Honors the threshold.

- Encourages surrender and trust.

The dying may still be able to respond to music so keep an eye on their body language and facial expressions. Even without words, your loved one may express through breath, facial tension, or movement whether the sounds are soothing for them or not. Pay attention to their presence. Let your intuition guide you, if something feels unsettled or unaligned, it may be time to pivot.

Humming

As the veil thins, the body and spirit may respond better to quiet presence rather than structured music. Humming can serve as soothing medicine for the dying providing comfort through tone and vibration. A soft hum creates a cocoon of sound that transforms the space into a sacred and timeless nest.

As we hum the gentle vibrations create soothing waves that resound throughout the body gifting an internal massage. As these waves unfold our minds begin to quiet, tension lessens in the body, and we anchor into the present moment.

When words are too much, or no longer accessible, humming offers a gentle, nonverbal way to connect with the dying person. The sweet hum of a familiar voice evokes a sense of solace while soothing the silence.

How to use humming as meditation for the dying

- Begin with presence.

- Sit or lay quietly with your loved one.

- Tune into their breath.

- Place one hand on your heart and the other on their hand or heart, if welcome.

- Choose a tune, tone, or mantra. No need for words. Just hum.

- Keep it slow and steady. Allow the hum to rise and fall with your own breath.

final rest eye pillow

DEATH CONTEMPLATION

YOU'LL NEED

Sewing machine or thread and needle for hand stitching, soft fabric, ruler, scissors, and rice. Optional additions: dried lavender, rose petals, or chamomile.

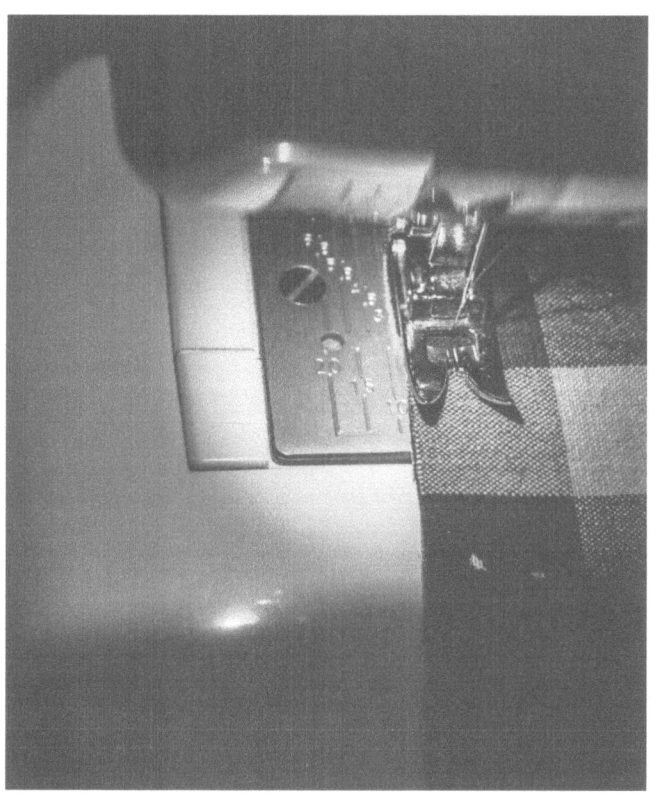

FINAL REST EYE PILLOW

An eye pillow is a simple sewn cloth pouch filled with rice and perhaps calming herbs. When placed gently over the eyes, it invites the nervous system to soften, our breath to deepen, and the outside world to fade. It becomes a ritual object that welcomes darkness, inwardness, silence, and stillness.

Darkness is not only the absence of light, but where dreams begin, visions unfold, and where we prepare to cross thresholds. The eye pillow helps soften the transition by signaling safety and surrender allowing the wearer to relax deeply and let go.

Making an eye pillow for yourself, a loved one, or someone preparing to die is a way to say: "May you *feel held. May you rest easy. May you find peace in the dark.*"

- Cut two rectangles of fabric, roughly 4 x 9 inches.

- Place the right sides of the fabric together and sew around three of the edges leaving the top open. Option to infuse your stitches with a silent prayer or intention: "*May this bring you rest.*"

- Fill with ¾ to 1 cup of rice (option to add dried petals)

- Sew final side of eye pillow with care and intention.

Corpse pose meditation

Begin by laying down in stillness, face up, and heart toward the sky. You may want to place a pillow or blanket under your head and under the backs of your knees.

When you are comfortable place your eye pillow gently over your eyes, as if laying down a soft veil between the seen and unseen. Let the weight of it guide you inward into the quiet space behind the eyes. Soften your eyelids. Release tension between your brows. Allow the backs of the eyes to soften.

Allow your arms to rest gently by your sides, with your palms face up. Let your legs fall away from each other naturally.

Breathe...

Inhale and exhale slowly... and let go...

Allow your breath to come into a natural rise and fall, as if the body is remembering how to dissolve into silence. Rest here...

Feel the ground beneath you, supporting you, and holding you. You are safe. You are home. This is not an ending, but a return, to the place before beginnings.

Let go of time. Let go of form.

Allow your bones to ground down. Allow the heaviness of your vessel to be your anchor. Let your muscles relax, letting go of any tension they hold on to. Let your skin soften and melt away.

Rest here for a few minutes.
You are free.

Eulogy

DEATH CONTEMPLATION

EULOGY

A eulogy is a goodbye in the expression of love and reminiscence for someone that died. It's a speech or a piece of writing that honors their life and consoles the bereaved. It is commonly told by friends or family as a way to celebrate, remember, and memorialize them. It is a way to tell a part of their story through our eyes. Giving a eulogy is an honor as well as a way to reflect on what you loved most about them.

There is no set timeframe to writing a eulogy. As grief moves with its own rhythm, so does the process of finding the words to honor a life. The words may flow in days, weeks, months, or even years after a death. What matters most is that the words flow truthfully and from the heart when it is shared.

Sharing a eulogy is a deeply vulnerable offering, one that may bring us down to our knees. When it feels right, if ever, these words can be shared in the presence of loved ones or kept sacred as an intimate expression of remembrance for ourselves. Feel into the timing and share when you are ready, if you choose unveil at all.

Soulful inquiries and reflections

- Tell us about your person. Tell us anything.
- What was their name, nickname, namesake?
- How did they live life?
- How did their love make you feel?
- What memory of them brings a smile to your face?
- What were their passions? Hopes? Dreams?
- Did you share any childhood memories?
- What songs remind you of them?
- Did they have a quote they lived by?
- How will you keep their spirit alive?
- How do you want them to be remembered and how will you share their story with others in the future?

My husband's eulogy

Brian Henry Rantz, my noble guy, best friend, partner, and person. He tended not to welcome just anybody to his side. But if he let you in, you knew him bone deep. He was a good man, unique, and at times misunderstood. Brian lived fast riding through countless battles and enduring many lives. His body was decorated with wounds and scars. He weathered many storms with unwavering strength as a man living by his own rules, often straying off the beaten path. He was brave, steadfast, and straightforward.

Brian embraced the outdoor lifestyle and called the streets home. He felt good after a ride. He once wrote, "ever since I saw this music video when I was laid up in a hospital bed, when I was a kid, of some guy rolling around a city on a bike with a backpack....I knew he was messengering....and I had the dream ever since." He fulfilled this dream alongside a beautiful community in the city. I beam with pride thinking of the man he became. I have a vivid memory of us, the night our love was renewed, we were walking back to his San Francisco apartment, he had his arm around my shoulders, his right hand holding my right hand, and he was walking his bicycle on the left side of his body.

I have always had eyes for this man. I was completely smitten from the start and even through the separation he was always the one I dreamed of. We traveled through life together. From age fourteen in strings class, to riding on the school bus and him gently kissing the top of my head, us slow dancing to Brown Eyed Girl together at senior prom, meeting up in Santa Monica in our twenties and him saying I saved his life, to in our thirties when I told him I wanted to get married and he said "I thought that since we were fourteen."

I grieve the loss of who he was, the old man he thought he'd be, and the husband that would walk me further into the future. Nevertheless, who he became was so much more beautiful than I could have ever imagined. He showed true strength in vulnerability, presence, and sacredness in surrender. When he allowed love in he felt safe and he softened with a heart broken open to the acceptance of the love he always deserved. I feel so lucky he chose me to walk him out. I will forever hold dear his gift of his last I love you and his final breath. We now continue to have a powerful connection beyond death and I look forward to embracing our transformation of relationship.

"Know my love shall never forsake you. I love you as before, as I always will. For no matter how far away you wander, you are my husband and I am your wife" - Starhawk.

Final Feelings

DEATH CONTEMPLATION

FINAL FEELINGS

Know that creation and death are sides of the same door, and honor that in your creative center.

Starhawk
The Pagan Book of Living and Dying

As I write this final piece I sit in sacred grief and presence. Brian died a little over five months ago. I can sit here and confidently say, he had the most beautiful death. More beautiful than I could have ever imagined.

A week before he died, his intake was next to nothing. As I tried to spoon feed him water he silently communicated to me "enough." The next day we did a water ceremony. The intention was to ask if intaking water had transitioned into harm instead of healing. The risk of aspiration became a deeper worry, and that was not the path his final days would take. The Animal Spirit card from the Wild Unknown deck we drew was the buffalo, its message, grounded yet heavenly, practical yet spiritual. It spoke of not fearing death...

The water ceremony consisted of three sips. He struggled to swallow each one and began reflective coughing, a protective way to stop the liquid getting into his lungs. I cradled his neck and head with trembling hands, gently kissed him on his forehead, and said this was our sign. Enough...

After three days of no water, contractions began and he entered into laboring death. Stronger medicine was called in to carry him gently though. I knew when mama medicine came into the death nest, that I would begin to loose him slowly, and that I did. At 4:44pm that evening, our anniversary, his wedding ring gently fell from his finger. His ring has stayed with mine on my hand ever since.

Shortly after, Brian became unresponsive and eyes at half mast. I asked our dear friend and death doula if he was sleeping or awake and she said she felt he was one foot on earth and the other in the heavens. The same message as the great buffalo card.

Before his passing, he was already whispering to me through signs from the in-between. One of the signs I asked for from him was 43. Our wedding date, April 3rd. As he lay dying 43's began to show on his oxygen and heart monitor, and if you've ever taken vitals before, you'd recognize these readings fall outside the norm. My love was already ascending. Body and mind earth-side, spirit in another realm.

On day seven, he began to yawn, an action he hadn't done all week. I knew he was preparing for his final breath. He went inward those 7 days. He was doing deep work using every ounce of life force that was left in his body. He gifted me his final breaths. They were slow, and sweet. He died with his mouth closed and a smile on his face.

I took my time with his body. I bathed him one final time, adorning every part of his vessel. I chose to have one last sleep with him in our bed, his death bed, knowing that he was no longer in his body. I watched his body become a shell, and with a deep knowing he was no longer in his body made it hard to sleep. Our doula and I adorned his vessel with flowers the next morning. And when I was ready, I called hospice letting them know I was open to receive support.

I always knew I wanted a slow and sacred bereavement. I was gifted the rare opportunity to grieve on my own time. I took time to walk through the difficult thresholds of returning to the world, making the calls, and closing what needed closing.

Grief revealed itself not only as sorrow, but as intense fear and anxiety. It became hard to leave the house, leave his remains, his urn. I developed a deep fear that our home would catch fire as I was away and I would lose him and his things all over again. But, I already lost him. And now I know that when that fear ignites, I name it. I hear him saying "enough" and I move on…. attempting to be as fearless as he was.

There is a feral knowing that as death touched me, I remain forever changed. I can feel the dark sorrow of his death flowing inside of me. It was a darkness of great depth, not of terror, but like the unseen parts of the deep well of descending into the heart, a place where light struggles to penetrate. I trust that though the path is veiled in shadows, one day this darkened tunnel will eventually end and light will release into my new world.

Slowly emerging out into the world I search for anchors to ground me back down to earth. Several creations from this book act as those anchors. Something to physically hold or look to to bring me back down. To calm my nervous system when I become anxious and overwhelmed when the world feels too normal and you don't seem to be on the same wavelength as everyone else right now.

I hope when death has touched you, forever changed you, and you feel alone… that your creations hold you as an anchor. That they serve you as much as your loved one. Because you are not alone.

You are never alone...

Today, I close another chapter of my grief journey. This is my last entry in this book we created side my side. Brian's birthday is tomorrow, and mine the next. We both would have been 38 years old. A few months ago, I received insight to end this writing journey alongside his birthday, a full circle moment. It felt like birthing our book into being, showing me that from death, something meaningful and tender could be born.

I chose to return to the same spot where we celebrated our birthdays the year before. As I approached, the ground was blanketed with yellow heart-shaped leaves. I sat with these pages before me, touching each one with the intention of release. When I finished, I bundled them with a silk ribbon and traced a sigil for letting go.

As I sat there crying, a gentle man approached. He didn't speak much English, so he opened a translator on his phone. He spoke softly into it, and turned the screen toward me. The message read... "He comes here often."

In that moment, I knew... it was a message from my beloved.

Tomorrow, the completed pages will be sent off for editing and publishing, closing this chapter with release. Then I will go to Lake Tahoe, to ride my bike among the waters edge and trees, holding his cremated remains (his bones) close to my chest in a travel urn, carried in the fanny pack he wore all the time. I will spend his first heavenly birthday, doing what he loved most, my way of honoring him on a day that aches with his absence.

As my final farewell to you, dear reader, I am deeply appreciative of being seen in this journey of being touched by death. Thank you for witnessing us. I imagine embracing each other, heart to heart, in reverence to being seen and soulfully seeing. This work serves as a legacy of love. It is a creation I feel deeply proud of and am eternally grateful for your presence.

The end... and the beginning...

IN GRATITUDE

Thank you, Mama, for being a mother to us both. For gathering us under your wing and offering a sanctuary of peace where Brian could live out his days in love and rest. Thank you for holding me as I held him.

To Sandra, my beautiful mother-in-law, thank you for gifting the world, and me, with Brian. Our Sunday connects continue to be such a beautiful way to keep his light shining between us. In your eyes, I see reflections of Brian's, and it fills me with such warmth.

Deep gratitude to my 5%, for seeing us fully, for standing with us through the most unguarded emotions and feral feelings, through loss, and for never wavering in your presence. We have felt truly seen, deeply nourished, and tenderly carried by your open hearts and watchful eyes.

Endless gratitude to our favorite hospice nurse, death doula, and forever friend, Katie. You have been a blessing and light in our lives. Your kindness, and the deep bond you shared with Brian, will remain forever etched in my heart. We are profoundly grateful for the way you stood beside us through the years and for guiding us toward a beautiful death.

Shirley, thank you for the love and devotion you poured into Brian's early years. Thank you for the care, safety, and devotion that held him as he grew, and for the childhood you gave him. I am endlessly grateful for all the photographs, small windows into his life, that I can return to again and again, holding him close in this way.

My deepest thanks to Brian's friends, the cycling community that knew him in the fullness of his life. Being with you on the memorial trip was one of my most cherished days. In each of you, I could see traces of Brian. In the way you moved, in what you wore, in the spirit you brought. It's a day I will always hold close.

To "The Vince", thank you for loving my beloved so deeply, both in high school and beyond. The connection you shared has touched me profoundly. The memories and stories you've shared are treasures I will carry with me always.

Thank you to all who have nourished us with meals, uplifted us with financial support, sat with us in presence, reached out through letters, or held us in love from afar. Every gesture has carried us.

To everyone who has ever created alongside me, thank you. Each shared moment of making has sparked inspiration for this book. Crafting has become my greatest outlet and companion while traveling through the death portal and path of grief.

To my editor, publisher, and soul sister, Sharissa, thank you. I am forever grateful for the connection we've woven together in this season of life and death. From your weekly presence, to nourishing us with food and love you shared, to the way you held space and walked this journey with me. You've been beside me through every step of this books creation. My gratitude for you runs endlessly deep.

BOOK RECOMMENDATIONS

The Gentle Art of Swedish Death Cleaning / Margareta Magnusson

No Death, No Fear / Thich Nhat Hanh

Hello, Goodbye / Day Schildkret

The Smell of Rain on Dust / Prechtel

Mary Magdalene Revealed / Meggan Watterson

Sacred Death / Hemali V. Vora

The Pagan Book of Living and Dying / Starhawk

Walking Each Other Home / Ram Dass

The Wild Edge of Sorrow / Francis Weller

Holding Space / Amy Wright Glenn

Signs / Laura Lynne Jackson

Death Nesting: Ancient & Modern Death Doula / Anne-Marie Keppel

The Eleventh Hour / Barbara Karnes

Brian Henry Rantz

9. 24. 1987 - 4. 7. 2025

Rachael Rantz is a widow, end of life doula, yoga practitioner, and sacred maker whose art took shape in the wake of loss. For four years, she served as a caregiver for her husband Brian through the slow progression of his terminal illness, walking with him through the sacred threshold of death. Bearing witness to each others vulnerability, grief, and presence opened the door for creativity to flow inside their death nest. Rachael birthed this book alongside her love as a way to prepare for the labor of death, loss, and bereavement. Through sharing a part of her story, she aspires to offer a glimmer of creative light to those deep in grief, reminding them that death can hold beauty, and that no one walks this path alone.